CELTIC MYTHOLOGY & HISTORY

Explore Timeless Tales, Folklore, Magic, Legendary Stories & More

HISTORY BROUGHT ALIVE

© Copyright 2022 - All rights reserved.

The content contained within this book may not be reproduced, duplicated, or transmitted without direct written permission from the author or the publisher.

Under no circumstances will any blame or legal responsibility be held against the publisher, or author, for any damages, reparation, or monetary loss due to the information contained within this book, either directly or indirectly.

Legal Notice:

This book is copyright protected. It is only for personal use. You cannot amend, distribute, sell, use, quote, or paraphrase any part, or the content within this book, without the consent of the author or publisher.

Disclaimer Notice:

Please note the information contained within this document is for educational and entertainment purposes only. All effort has been executed to present accurate, up-to-date, reliable, complete information. No warranties of any kind are declared or implied. Readers acknowledge that the author is not engaged in the rendering of legal, financial, medical, or professional advice. The content within this book has been derived from various sources. Please consult a licensed professional before attempting any techniques outlined in this book.

By reading this document, the reader agrees that under no circumstances is the author responsible for any losses, direct or indirect, that are incurred as a result of the use of the information contained within this document, including, but not limited to, errors, omissions, or inaccuracies.

FREE BONUS FROM HBA: EBOOK BUNDLE

Greetings!

First of all, thank you for reading our books. As fellow passionate readers of History and Mythology, we aim to create the very best books for our readers.

Now, we invite you to join our VIP list. As a welcome gift, we offer the History & Mythology Ebook Bundle below for free. Plus you can be the first to receive new books and exclusives! <u>Remember it's 100% free to join.</u>

Simply scan the QR code to join.

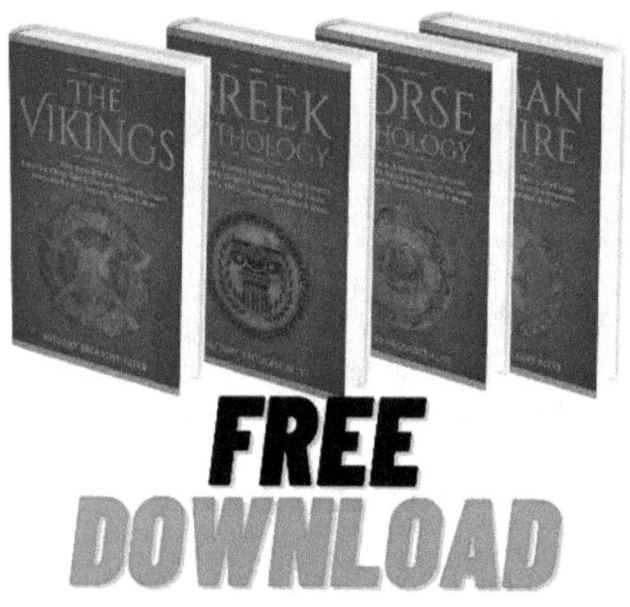

Keep up to date with us on:
YouTube: History Brought Alive
Facebook: History Brought Alive
www.historybroughtalive.com

CONTENTS

INTRODUCTION 1

CHAPTER 1: CELTIC ORIGINS AND HISTORY 4

CHAPTER 2: CELTIC TRADITIONS 20

CHAPTER 3: CELTIC RELIGION AND RITUALS 29

CHAPTER 4: CELTIC DEITIES 38

CHAPTER 5: CELTIC CREATURES 63

CHAPTER 6: CELTIC FOLKTALES 81

    CONNLA AND THE FAIRY MAIDEN 82
    THE HORNED WOMEN 86
    BREWERY OF EGGSHELLS 90

CHAPTER 7: CELTIC COSMOLOGY 93

CHAPTER 8: CELTIC OGHAM 117

CONCLUSION: CELTS OF THE PRESENT 138

REFERENCES 145

INTRODUCTION

As one of the most powerful people to dominate some influential parts of Europe, it comes as no surprise that there is an ever-growing interest in the history and mythology of the Celts.

However, this interest can be somewhat stunted by a lack of clear historical materials. The intellectuals of the Celtic culture—called *druids*—believed that if you didn't make an effort in remembering, then you would become "soft in the head" (Paxton, 2019). This was the reason for their disapproval of writing, in addition to the druids' desire to control sacred lore without enabling outsiders to have access to it.

Although the extent of this ancient Iron Age European culture is made unclear by this lack of written records, a fascination is fueled by archeological studies and classical accounts that make up a basic understanding of the origins, religion, traditions, and tales shared among the Celts.

This manuscript brings together both the facts and folklore of the Celtic world. You will read about the historical context of these powerful people and learn more about ancient Celtic communities. In addition, your mind will be filled with the curious tales told over centuries, leading up to their modern-day significance.

As the director, George Lucas once said, "I've come to the conclusion that mythology is really a form of archaeological psychology. Mythology gives you a sense of what a people believe, what they fear," (n.d.). By enlightening yourself on Celtic history and mythology, you also form a cultural understanding of the present-day Celtic descendants. While the ancient Celts evolved around 1200 BCE, primarily in parts of western Europe—involving their migration between modern-day Britain, France, Ireland, and Spain—their culture remains most prominent in Ireland and Great Britain.

Unfortunately, Greek and Roman authors were biased against any non-Greeks or non-Romans and were liable to use stereotypical perceptions and criticism when discussing Celtic culture. As a result, most texts about Celts are not particularly realistic or objective, but should not be altogether discredited. There are very few—mainly fragmented—inscriptions by the Celts themselves, thus historians are forced to rely on the images created by ancient Greek and Roman texts.

This manuscript holds interesting information gathered from a wide variety of sources and is intended to bring the Celts back to life. Every chapter is clearly set out and speaks about everything including where the Celts came from, their essential ceremonies, the gods they praised, the creatures they feared, the stories told during centuries-old bedtimes, Celtic magic, the Celtic descendants, and everything in between.

Let's dive into the wonderful world of Celtic culture.

CHAPTER 1
CELTIC ORIGINS AND HISTORY

While it is uncertain what the Celts called themselves, "Celtic" is a modern reference to tribes that inhabited parts of western Europe and regions near the Danube River during the Iron Age, from 1200–600 BCE.

After the earliest evidence of Celtic looting—of Delphi in 279 BCE—the ancient Greek geographer, Strabo, recorded a meeting in 335 BCE between them and Alexander the Great in the Balkans. From writings such as these, we can determine that the Celtic tribes were known as "Galatia, Keltai, or Keltoi" to the Greeks, whereas the Romans referred to them as "Celtae, Celti, Galli, or Gauls" (Amgueddfa Cymru, 2021). These terms translate to 'barbarian' or 'foreigner'. Interestingly, the term 'Gaul' was ironically transferred into the Celtic languages over time and 'gall' is still used today to refer to an outsider. For example, Gall Baile (anglicized as Galbally, Co. Limerick, Ireland) means "town of the foreigner" in reference to Anglo-Saxon colonizers.

The first mention of the people who lived north of the Greek colony of Massalia, in Gaul—using the term 'Celt'—was seen in the written records by the Greek author, Hecataeus of Miletus from 517 BCE. Hecataeus' work is only known through extracts by later Greek authors.

However, Roman authors provided more valuable insight as they had direct contact with the European tribes as the Roman world expanded.

While ancient historians were uncertain about the geographical accuracy of the Celts—mainly because many authors who wrote about them never traveled to their supposed territories and based their writings on rumors—traces of Celtic settlements have been discovered as far as central and eastern France, southern Germany, and the Czech Republic.

The poet, Avienus, wrote an interesting poem in 400 CE called *Ora Maritima*. This text also included information by the Carthaginian author, Himilco, who wrote about a voyage into

Celtic territory around 500 BCE. Writings such as these guide current historians to form more reliable and well-rounded opinions on the Celts and their descendants.

There are allegedly six Celtic nations according to the remnants of the language, including Cornwall, Brittany, the Isle of Man, Ireland, Scotland, and Wales.

Celts were associated with traits that often described them as barbaric. Plato ridiculed the Celts for drunkenness, while his student, Aristotle, wrote that they showed a sense of crazed fearlessness. These opinions, however, reveal little of the actual ancient Celtic culture. In this regard, archaeological and anthropological finds prove far more informative.

Roughly 3,000 years ago, the Russian steppes—an area of unforested grassland—started to wither due to climate change. The area experienced drought, crops failed, and the settlers were forced to migrate west. By 800 BCE, in central Europe, societies emerged as the Iron Age's developments became inexorable. Archeologists of the 1900s found that an area in Austria, called Hallstatt, introduced the first period of Celtic development preceding the Le Tène period. The area's importance lay in the salt rock mountains that surrounded the village. Salt was essential in the preservation of meat and used in trade. The eighth century BCE introduced salt mining in this region, where the mine output was valued far more than the miners' lives. Excavations have uncovered perfectly preserved pieces of clothing, miners' axes, horn drinking cups, pieces of leather, miners' rucksacks, tasseled miners' caps, and skeletal remains.

From such evidence, it is believed that the miners spent days working, eating, and sleeping inside the mines, and sadly, many lives were taken by the frequent mining disasters. The site was finally closed down by a mudslide, creating molded figures as the mud filled the cavities left inside the cave. Archeologists were able to use these figures and determine what—and who— were buried in the mudslide. It is believed that these workers were mainly slaves, and besides the salt, those who traded with the Greeks for precious goods often offered these slaves as payment.

Additionally, archeologists discovered over 1,000 graves of the more fortunate ancient people of the area. Though this does not give us insight into the daily lives of the early Celts, other than the potential hazards that they may have faced, burial rituals provide huge cultural clues as to the beliefs and mythology of the group. Some of these graves held individual skeletal remains while others held couples. Cremated remains were also discovered inside elaborate bronze vessels. While men's lives were short, anthropological evidence indicates that women's death rates were highest between the ages of 13 and 26. This was due to frequent deaths during childbirth.

After the Hellenization—where non-Greek regions were made "more Greek"—the main Greek colony that spread into the Celtic territories was Massalia. This colony was established around 600 BCE near the mouth of the Rhône river. Massalia was then still surrounded by Celts during the Le Tène period (discussed further in Chapter 2). By 300 BCE, it was believed that the Celts—described in the classic text as fair-haired, muscular, and tall—dominated most of the European regions north of the Alps. Classical authors also wrote about the Celts wearing brightly-colored wool clothing and using the woad plant (*Isatis tinctoria*) to make blue dye and paint markings on their bodies. Celts' clothing incorporated a tunic with a belt and sometimes a cloak and trousers that were fastened with a brooch (or *fibula*). Many historians argue that the Celts were some of the first nations to wear trousers. This later developed into including the use of Scottish Tartan per the individual's important status within the tribe.

By 200 BCE, the Celts started to utilize the Greek alphabet in Gallic inscriptions. This is around the time when the classic author Strabo describes Massalia as a school for 'barbarians'. For many years, it was believed that the Celts served as mercenary soldiers through the Mediterranean, invading regions in Italy due to "piqued curiosity" in Italian luxuries, Greece for its Massaliote wealth, and the Rhône because of the cultivation of wine (Witt, 1997).

Under the reign of Julius Caesar, which started in 100 BCE, the ancient Romans initiated a crusade against the Celts, allowing the Celtic culture only to survive on the islands of Europe's western coast. Thousands of Celts were murdered during Rome's military campaign and their culture was eliminated throughout most of the European mainland. Caesar's armies also attempted to invade Britain and Ireland but were fortunately unsuccessful, enabling the Celts to make it their eventual homeland.

This condensing of the Celts into a smaller geographical area meant that several ethnicities formed the Celtic nation, including the Britons, the Gaels, the Galatians, the Gauls, and the Irish.

Those who lived in Brittany were known as *The Britons*. This northwestern corner of France was occupied by Gauls as well, and its isolation enabled their traditions to survive by being cut off from the rest of France. French "Bretons" often wear *coiffes*—a traditional Celtic hat made of lace—and nearly one-quarter of Brittany's population speaks the Celtic language, Breton, which sounds similar to Welsh.

Although it is difficult to trace where the Celtic language originated from, it is believed that it was derived from an ancient language called "proto-Indo-European" (Amgueddfa Cymru, 2021). Linguists assume that people introduced this language to western Europe by traveling from central Asia during 6000–2000 BCE. The earliest Celtic language inscriptions date back to the sixth century BCE and were discovered in northern Italy. While today, Celtic languages are mainly spoken on the Atlantic facade of Europe—particularly Britain and Ireland—it was once a prominent language in the regions of western and central Europe. This was until the fall of the Roman Empire around 476 CE.

A study from 1707 CE, conducted by Edward Lhuyd, defined two Celtic language groups. This involves P-Celtic—also called *Brythonic*—consisting of Breton, Cornish, and Welsh, and Q-Celtic—also called *Goidelic*—that consists of Irish, Manx, and Scots Gaelic. As suggested by the 16th-century scholar, George Buchanon, all Europeans once spoke a relation of Gallic languages. Whereas P-Celtic languages likely came from Gaul (France), Q-Celtic languages would have been from Iberia (Spain and Portugal).

The Celtic language used in *Cymru*—what we know as Wales—is Welsh. Whereas, in Cornwall, very few individuals speak Cornish, which was developed from Welsh and Breton. In Scotland, there is a minority that still speaks the Celtic language Scots Gaelic, and more commonly, cultural practices rooted in ancient Celtic origins are seen in bagpipes and some Scottish dances. Similar to this, the Celtic descendants in Ireland also used to speak a form of Gaelic. Both the Romans and Anglo-Saxons failed to conquer Ireland, enabling the survival of the Gaels and the Celtic Irish. However, the use of Irish Gaelic started to lessen in the 1600s CE with the British introduction of the Penal Laws banning the use of the Irish language as a means of cultural control. It is only in recent decades that the use of this language has begun to recover in Ireland as citizens aim to reclaim their Celtic roots.

Other Celtic regions, unfortunately, were colonized—both physically and culturally—much earlier in history, leading to a degradation of their Celtic culture. Caesar's armies successfully invaded Brittany before his murder, forcing the Britons to migrate west toward Cornwall and Wales, and north to Scotland. Thereafter, the Romans erected *Hadrian's Wall* near the England-Scotland border to protect themselves against the Celts, which ironically helped to protect the integrity of Scottish Celts, giving us much more archaeological and linguistic evidence of their culture than is found, for instance, in Cornwall.

The Celts who resided in Spain were referred to as *The Galatians*. They occupied most of the Asturias region—now known as northern Spain—where they often fought off Roman and Moorish invasions. Some Galatians also lived in the present-day northwest coast of Spain, previously called Galacia. There is evidence that supports their former residence in the area, such as Galatian descendants that still take part in ancient outdoor dances while playing bagpipes. The regional flag is also adorned with a Celtic symbol similar to the "Celtic cross" called *Cruz de la Victoria*.

However, in general, Celtic cultural practices were largely at risk of overwhelm by outside forces. During the conquest of Gaul in 100 BCE, the Romans stole treasures from the Celtic temples. Though some Celtic gods were adopted by the Romans, most figures in temples were replaced by those of Roman gods. Once the invaders achieved more control over the Celts, the Roman Empire took measures to eradicate the Celtic cultural leaders, in this case, the druids. Druidism became prohibited and prominent sanctuaries—such as Anglesey—were destroyed.

Late antiquity—before Christianity spread through Europe—brought a revival of the Celtic religion as the Roman Empire fell. Some of the ancient Celtic gods survived into unconquered Ireland, Scotland, and Wales, where they were adapted into contemporary versions that were mainly venerated as humanized hero figures in literature, and sometimes adopted into Hiberno-Christianity as saints. Unfortunately, though, for the most part, the ancient Celtic religion was a victim of conquests and was never the same again.

Due to the numerous ethnicities within the

Celtic culture, there was considerable variance in Celtic lifestyles, practices, and traditions. However, the importance of warfare and its traditions were important among all Celtic societies from the Hallstatt culture (c. 1200 BCE) to the La Tène culture (c. 500 BCE). Like all cultures, war was presented in art, religion, and social structures, especially since the Celts were credited with a warrior reputation among their counterparts of the ancient world. Although it is argued that the Celts weren't as organized as some societies of the time, they possessed great skill in working bronze, gold, and iron. Many technical and metalwork innovations also emerged from the Celtic culture.

While little is definitively known about the Celts, and the majority of our sources are from biased classical text, archeological discoveries have led to valuable information regarding a Celtic hierarchical structure, including warrior status and prestige's influence on the aristocracy. It is evident from early Irish literature that different social classes, including the noblemen, the free people, and the slaves, existed within Celtic communities. Clientship was essential in these societies. Patrons offered financial support, hospitality, and protection to their followers, who in turn provided their loyalty in battle, labor, and products from their farms. This practice, along with raiding and warfare, allowed individuals to improve their social standing. Therefore, the two most important sources of wealth—cattle and treasure—were often stolen during the many raids. As some raids were intended to conquer nearby communities and political power, this caused a violent and forceful subjugation under the kings and chieftains of Celtic Europe.

The importance of prestige is also noted in many Proto-Celtic and Celtic burials—that date back to 1200 BCE—when influential individuals were buried with objects of warfare. Termed the 'Urnfield' culture, these graves were distinguished from the rest by the riches and significant burial rites. The most wealthy were buried with objects such as horse gear, weapons, carts, and wagons, that acted as precursors to chariots in later European wars and rites (King, 2019).

This significance was shared by the Hallstatt culture and the La Tène that followed. However, the Hallstatt burial sites introduced other important objects, like horns used as drinking cups, and the ability to host lavish feasts became a primary indication of status. The La Tène burials contained helmets, shields, spears, swords, and objects used during feasts.

Burials such as these not only make us aware of the prestige of warriorhood in Celtic society but also have presented us with much insight into the battle regalia that was used at the time. Celtic shields were elongated oval-shaped plates that were often adorned with bronze and iron motifs, for example, the *Battersea Shield*. The Celts' swords were worn on their hips from an iron chain. Light spears were thrown from horseback, while larger ones were called *lanciae*. Very few, oddly-shaped, helmets were excavated from fifth-century La Tène graves. This suggests that the Celts did not often wear helmets in battle and instead, used them during ceremonies. This evidence is compounded by Greek and Roman authors who also wrote that the Celts "scorned the use of helmets" (King, 2019). The only helmets were discovered in Italy. Ceremonial helmets were made of expensive materials such as coral, bronze, and gold. Rather than protection, the helmets were ornate and shaped to make the wearer stand out at a parade.

While the practice of burying the elite with wagons and chariots was mainly limited to central Europe in Bohemia and Germany, burials that held horse gear, ornate helmets, shields, and weapons were discovered to have spread to as far as Britain and Ireland.

The *Gundestrup Cauldron* from Jutland, Denmark, likewise presents a warrior hierarchy. It also depicts the belief in the afterlife and how that could advance social status. The bottom register shows a row of spearmen marching toward a god—presumably associated with war—followed by a man wearing a boar-crested helmet with a sword in his hand, and three *carnyx*—an instrument used to increase noise and confusion on the battlefield—players behind him. The top register shows a man dipped into a cauldron of rebirth by the war god, while a row of chieftains rides away from the god on horseback.

In addition to these artifacts, the later legends of the Celts also provide much insight into their society. The Ulster Cycle—also called the Irish Ulaid Cycle—refers to the literature group of legends about the heroic age of the Ulaids. The Ulaids were from northeast Ireland and inspired the modern name of the province of Ulster. Their stories are set in 100 BCE and recorded from 800–1100 CE. The Ulster Cycle is reflective of a pre-Christian aristocracy that fought from chariots, allegedly took the heads of their enemies as trophies, and was influenced by druids and geasa.

The events of the time revolve around the reign of King Conor—*Conchobar mac Nessa*—and his knights of the Red Branch at Emain Macha (present-day Navan Center and Fort, Co. Armagh). The Red Branch—*An Cróeb Derg*—was supposedly the palace where the severed heads and limbs of their enemies were stored. Its hero was Cú Chulainn—the son of King Conor's mortal sister and the god, *Lugh*. King Conor's rival was King Ailill and his goddess Queen Medb in Connaught. Most of the Ulster Cycle legends speak of cattle raids, elopements, and destructions, with the best-known epic being *The Cattle Raid of Cooley*.

Classic texts speak of Celts riding both chariots and wagons into battle to intimidate their enemies before attacking them. Caesar describes the scene (1869):

[The Britons'] mode of fighting with their chariots is this: Firstly, they drive about in all directions and throw their weapons and generally break the ranks of the enemy with the very dread of their horses and the noise of their wheels; and when they have worked themselves in between the troops of horse, leap from their chariots and engage on foot. (Gal., 4.33)

By 100 BCE, the use of chariots in the continental European wars began to phase out, being replaced by mounted warriors. However, due to their isolation, regions of Britain and Ireland continued to use chariots up until around 83 CE.

As the Celtic tribes flourished in Britain and Ireland, it allowed for many traditions to develop and set their culture aside from others.

CHAPTER 2
CELTIC TRADITIONS

Many variations of Celtic practices existed across their different regions for numerous centuries. However, key features remained the same.

Aside from the little-known facts about the belief in life after death—evident in the food, ornaments, and weapons often buried with the deceased—the Celtic doctrine involved the druid teachings of reincarnation and the 'otherworld' where there was no illness, old age, sadness, or death. This alternative existence was either imagined as underground or on islands in the ocean. Celts referred to the otherworld as "the delightful plain," "the land of the living," or *Tír na nÓg*—"the land of the young" (Dillon & Mac Cana, 1999). This otherworld was similar to the Greek belief of Elysium.

Celtic eschatology—beliefs concerning

death—speaks of a beautiful woman singing of the otherworld (*shee*) as she approaches the hero. When he decides to follow her, they sail away on a glass boat. It is also believed that in this world, time passes differently. There are 100 years in the mortal realm during just one day in the otherworld, thus, when the hero returns—such as in the legend of *Oisín*—everyone he knew is long dead.

If the hero is sent on a quest, a magic mist appears around him, and he is welcomed by a beautiful woman and a warrior into a palace. The warrior is either *Manannán* or *Lugh* (discussed in Chapter 4) who sends the hero on a strange adventure, from which he successfully returns.

The Gaulish religion was the responsibility of three authoritative classes, namely druids, *filídh* (bards), and *vates* (seers). The name 'druid' is translated to "knowing the oak tree" (Dillon & Mac Cana, 1999). This relates to their rituals that mostly took place in forest sanctuaries before the Gallo-Roman period—the Romanization of Gauls—introduced temples. According to Caesar, the druids had many privileges, such as paying no taxes and avoiding manual labor. However, druids had to learn all verses by heart—as they were opposed to writing them down—and spent nearly 20 years studying.

Apart from these oral histories, Caesar, Cicero, Lucan, and Suetonius all mention that human sacrifice took place in Gaul, and Pliny the Elder noted its occurrence in Britain too. The practice was forbidden under Claudius and Tiberius, and some evidence suggests that known human sacrifice in Ireland was banned by St. Patrick who is said to have favored ritualistic banishment.

Moreover, the importance of archaeological finds remains prevalent. The Bull Rock Caves in Moravia, Czech Republic, became a point of interest after archeological excavations revealed more about the site's history, dating back to roughly 600 BCE. The site held artifacts from numerous cultures across Europe, including armor, bronze belts associated with northern Italy, Celtic statues, ceramics, Baltic amber and glass beads, jewelry, a Neolithic cave painting, Caucasus-region iron weaponry, and textiles. A fireplace was also discovered inside the cave, in addition to jars that still held millet and meat. At the far end, archeologists found the remains of a Celtic Iron Age metal workshop with tools. Many of these artifacts are currently located in the Museum of Natural History in Vienna,

Austria.

Many artistic innovations like metalwork and stone carving were accredited to the Celts across Europe. Elaborate artifacts of bronze, gold, silver, and precious stones can be viewed in Celtic museum collections throughout Europe and North America.

Upon its initial investigation in 1867 by a local doctor, named Jindřich Wankel, the Bull Rock Caves showed signs of Paleolithic, Eneolithic, Hallstatt, La Tène, and Medieval settlement for short periods. In 1869, two explorers found a Celtic statue of a bronze bull dating back to 560 BCE. This discovery piqued interest and during a two-month excavation of the entrance hall in 1872, nearly 40 human bodies—mainly men and women aged 30 to 45—were uncovered. Some bodies were missing their heads, hands, and feet. There were also skeletal remains of horses.

Many believe that these were part of sacrificial rituals. On a stone altar, two severed arms wearing bracelets and rings were placed next to a split skull on a bed of grain stalks. Remnants of three gold-fitted chariots and the remains of a man—assumed to have been a Celtic chieftain—were uncovered deeper in the cave. However, the nature behind this mass grave remains unclear, as anthropologists have failed to determine whether these individuals were murdered or sacrificed. While some wounds indicate to have been fatal, many appear post-mortem. Uncovering the truth was further complicated after any remaining evidence was buried under concrete during World War II when the Germans paved the Bull Rock Cave for the use of a weapons facility.

From historical sites such as this, it can be determined that a new style of art appeared during 400 BCE and spread across Europe. Archeologists argue that this art style is evident in common Celtic culture. The majority of Celtic art was identified and analyzed by British scholars during the 1850s. However, it was only around 1910 that this art style was traced to the areas of northeast France, southern Germany, and the Czech Republic. Following the discovery of decorated metalworks on the edge of Lake Neuchâtel in Switzerland, the art style was named La Tène. While the spread of La Tène art was interpreted as Celtic invasions, historians recently became dissatisfied with that idea due to the lack of conclusive evidence.

Archeological discoveries of the Iron Age in Britain suggest there were various regional societies with their own distinctive identities.

After reconsidering their assumptions, archeologists argue that while La Tène art was found in Wales, this does not indicate Celtic invasion, instead suggesting the spread and exchange of fashion across societies.

Furthermore, we know from these sources that animals took a prominent place under the Celts, especially horses. Although horses were domesticated in Europe and used as track animals centuries before, the Celts were some of the first to master the skills of horse riding. They were renowned for this skill. The horse became essential in Celtic livelihood, war, and religion. The Spartan general Pausanias (c. 110 BCE) spoke of a war tactic called *trimarcisia*. This involved mounted warriors who would be accompanied by two stablemen with their horses who would act as substitutes in their master's place if he was wounded. One stableman would return his master home while the other joined in battle.

Regarding the Celtic perception of the passage of time, the Celtic year in Ireland consisted of two six-month periods that were divided by the feasts of *Bealtaine* (first of May) and *Samhain* (first of November). Furthermore, these two periods were equally divided by the feast of *Imbolc* (first of February) and

Lughnasadh (first of August). Although *Samhain* originally meant "summer," the festival marked the last day of summer, resulting in *Samhain* now being the modern standard Irish language term for the month of November. *Bealtaine* was also called *Cétsamain*, meaning "first Samhain" (Dillon & Mac Cana, 1999). The French scholar, Joseph Vendryes, compared *Imbolc* to Roman lustrations because it was a purification ceremony for farmers. This was connected to the lambing season, and was sometimes also called *oímelc*, meaning "sheep milk." *Bealtaine*—which translated to "fire of Beil"—was the summer festival during which druids drove cattle between two fires to protect them all against illness, and *Lughnasadh* was the feast in honor of the Celtic god, Lugh. Likewise, for each of the feasts mentioned, the Celts celebrated with the gods Beil (*Bealtaine*), Brigid (*Imbolc*), and Tlachtga (*Samhain*). These festivals are still known by their ancient Celtic names in Ireland.

Pagans and druids used a natural calendar according to the alignment of the ancient passage *cairns*—like Newgrange, meaning "new farm"—with four bright stars from the "belt of the Zodiac" (Connor & Connor, 2020). Equinoxes and solstices do not align with the stars, instead, they represent the turning points of the day-night balance. The Celtic New Year starts on the new—referred to as the 'dark'—moon of *Samhain*. It is believed that the lack of direct solar and reflected lunar light allows the Earth goddess to give birth to the new year. The Celtic New Year ceremony also included all the druids in Ireland putting out old flames, igniting a pure flame at Tlachtga hill that was taken to Tara's High King and distributed to the representatives of tribes to take a pure flame back to their communities.

The true traditional *Samhain* is celebrated at the end and beginning of a new year, as a way of honoring the dead because the festival is intended to celebrate both death and rebirth.

Considering the natural Celtic calendar—that determines the solstice according to sidereal—the winter solstice starts when the sunrise over Lambay Volcano aligns with the Sagittarius star at 30° or Capricorn star at 0°. For example, in 2005, this sidereal event took place on December 21 at 18:37. Whereas in 2006, it happened on December 22 at 00:24. As Niamh Connor explains (2020):

The Celtic and pre-Celtic festivals are aligned to the Sun rising with a specific degree of the Belt of the Zodiac in the background and this is shown with two markers i.e. the Belt of the Zodiac and the East of North coordinates. (p.8)

The Celtic festivals based on the solar alignment over Lambay Volcano are as follows:

- *Imbolc* is at 10° with Aquarius
- Spring equinox is at 0° with Aries
- *Bealtaine* is at 10° with Taurus
- Summer solstice is at 0° with Cancer
- *Lughnasa* is at 10° with Leo
- Autumn equinox is at 0° with Libra
- *Samhain* is at 10° with Scorpio

As mentioned, *Samhain* is the start of the Celtic new year. This is the last of the fire festivals, where animals were slaughtered, hides were tanned, meat was smoked, and the careful selection of stock for the coming year was finalized. Fire pits were used to burn animal offal and fight the flies hunting the foul smells. *Samhain* is contemporarily referred to as Halloween, Catholic All Saints Day, Wiccan Great Sabbat, and Hindu Diwali.

CHAPTER 3
CELTIC RELIGION AND RITUALS

The Celts followed a polytheistic religion—worshiping more than one god—and while their beliefs varied across eras and locations, the Celtic religion generally had high regard for natural sites, such as sacred groves and rivers. Ritualistic events incorporated votive offerings to their gods, often in the form of food or animal sacrifice. Additionally, the Celts commemorated the deceased by placing valuable objects in the tombs of their loved ones.

Hardly any sacred Celtic text or hymns exists, because their religion was led by druids who were opposed to writing down their knowledge. This adds to the gaps in our understanding of the origin, universe, and fate that the Celts viewed for themselves.

Nonetheless, a sensible idea of the religious

practices and pre-Christian European beliefs is created by a combination of Celtic artifacts, studies, and methodologies.

The druids were considered the religious leaders and intermediaries between Celtic humanity and the gods. They were known for their vast knowledge of Celtic traditions and wisdom.

Aside from managing religious rituals, druids provided practical assistance in their societies by interpreting events of nature, acting as soothsayers, and producing medicine from sacred plants, such as mistletoe. Druids were the repositories of Celtic history and likely cast *geassa*—or spells—to ensure compliance with the society's rules and religious inclusion. There is hardly any evidence that suggests women acted as druids, but nothing suggests that they were not allowed to take on the role.

Druids received high status in Celtic societies and presumably highlighted their roles by wearing white robes and unusual headgear with antler attachments. As mentioned before, fully-practicing druids had to train for 20 years. There was an emphasis on oral learning and no written records were taken.

On the other hand, Roman writers

frequently misinterpreted the role of druids. For example, future divination was often described as the role of a separate class of individuals, called seers. Seers were responsible for interpreting natural phenomena, like the flight patterns of certain birds.

Druids were also often equated to *filídh*, the learned poets of ancient Ireland. It is still debated by scholars whether druids, seers, and *filídh* are separate individuals or the roles of one person.

Druids gathered in their sacred locations during annual events, evident in Julius Caesar's *Gallic Wars*, where he describes such a sacred site in central France where the Carnutes tribe resided. Similarly, Mona—Anglesey, Wales—was also a well-known holy island for druids before the first century CE.

In 432 CE, when St. Patrick introduced Ireland to Christianity, many ancient Celtic traditions were adapted into this "new religion" (History.com Editor, 2019). Catholicism became the dominant religion on the island after most Druids were murdered, but traces of Celtic culture remained in the prominence of a new religion. The shamrock—a symbol commonly associated with Ireland—presumably represents the "Holy Trinity" of

Catholicism (Roach, 2010). Whereas many see the Celtic cross as an adaptation of the Catholic cross. Furthermore, *Imbolc*—the festival of the Celtic goddess Brigid—was adapted to become St. Bridget's Day, still celebrated on the first of February in Ireland to this day.

Bogs, lakes, and rivers were held as important sites by the Celts. It is believed that water was considered a conduit to the 'otherworld' (as discussed in Chapter 2). Therefore, the junctions of rivers and springs were especially sacred. Rituals were also held on hilltops, mountains, and in oak tree groves, called *nemeton*. Community elders also frequently gathered under the shade of large single oak trees. These were the meeting places between the physical and supernatural realms.

Sacred sites were prepared by use of purpose-built earthworks, gates, shrines, or temples. They presumably also used monolithic structures to develop their distinctive style involving a rectangular ditched enclosure. This is referred to as *Viereckschanzen* since many were initially discovered in southern Germany, although they are also found at Celtic sites across the regions from Bohemia to France. The space was given an outer ditch-like earthwork and a gate on the east side. A bare sacred area contained wooden poles to support the roofed structures and for the carving of votive symbols and imagery. Deep shafts were also incorporated, where offerings were deposited, such as pottery that dates back to as far as 200 BCE.

Stone temples were first utilized by the Celts around 400 BCE, and these were typically given monumental doorways that were adorned with paintings and carvings. The roofs were made of intertwined branches or thatch covered with clay and lime.

The Celts believed that the head was the basis of one's soul, and resultantly, masks were often used as decoration in temples. Some argue that the heads of human sacrifices were also used, but this is debated. The Roman conquest introduced classical architecture and design features. Sacred sites were filled with tall wooden statues and artwork that represented the gods. The figures were often featureless and wore metal torcs—stiff necklaces often embellished with twisting designs. Celtic gods were scarcely represented in stone.

As mentioned in Chapter 2, rituals were held under the cycles of nature and astronomy, and scheduled based on the phases of the moon. These rituals involved incantations and votive offerings to appease the gods. It was intended to thank them and gain their favor for future events. A common subject was the avoidance of disaster, drought, famine, and losing a war. Thus, these offerings would include food, jewelry, armor, weaponry, and pottery. Those who were recovering from an illness made small models of themselves—or those suffering—and the affected part of the body, which was then sacrificed to the gods.

It was common to bend or break the objects during these rituals, as is seen in the many goods thrown into the waters at sacred sites near bogs, lakes, and rivers. An excavation that took place at Anglesey found broken cauldrons, animal bones, decorative metal pieces—presumably part of chariots and riding gear, slave chains and collars, swords, shields, and spear points. Animals were sacrificed by burning or burying them intact at the sacred site. These included bulls, dogs, horses, and oxen. Evidence suggests that parts of the animal were feasted on before the rest were offered to the gods.

It is believed that a rarer occurrence was that of human sacrifice. These presumably only happened at times of severe stress to the community, for example during a war or natural disaster. The individuals who were sacrificed were more likely to be the captured enemy warriors. Although this is debated by many scholars, a possible sacrificial victim was *Lindow Man* who appears to have died around the start of 200 CE. This corpse was discovered at Lindow Moss near Cheshire, England, and shows evidence of typical ritual killings, involving a blow to the head, strangulation, a cut-throat, and being put in water for some time before burying the body at the sacred site.

According to Roman writers, human sacrifice was sometimes specific to a selected god. For example, sacrifice victims for Esus hung from a tree while their limbs were removed, those for Taranis were burnt alive, and Teutates required his victims to be drowned (discussed further in Chapter 4). The Roman author Strabo (c. 64 BCE - 24 CE) wrote of an elaborate method involving a large figure built of wood and straw, then set on fire after it was filled with cattle, wild animals, and humans (Amgueddfa Cymru, 2021).

These sacrifices were believed to also foresee future events. Elements such as the direction of their blood flow and the examination of their entrails were all scrutinized for signs after a victim's death.

The Celts strongly believed in an afterlife. The graves of elite individuals and leaders were filled with their personal possessions, such as armor, board games, clothing, food, paraphernalia for feasts, precious objects, and weapons. The individual's importance was highlighted by being placed in a wood-lined chamber that was deposited into a large mound of earth. The inner chamber held the finely-dressed corpse that was often placed on a dismantled four-wheeled wagon or bench. However, burials in flat graves gradually started to replace the use of mounds.

The practice of burying the deceased with objects suggested that they believed the dead will use them on the journey to and when they are in the afterlife. The otherworld was interpreted as similar to the Celtic mortal world but without any negative elements like pain and sorrow. The Celts believed that there was little to fear from death. Aside from being buried, some Celts were also cremated and then buried. Cremation increased in popularity during 200 BCE and onward. Historians argue that this was due to the influence of Mediterranean cultures.

The Celts believed in many sources of protection. One, in particular, was amulets. These were considered to protect both the living and the dead on their journeys through the mortal- and other-world. Amulets were presented in many forms, including miniature axes, feet, shoes, or wheels. It was believed that amulets would ward off dangers—contradictory to talismans which lead to bad luck—and were mainly uncovered in the graves of women and children.

The introduction of Christianity in the fifth century had a profound impact on the Celtic religion. Unfortunately, the earliest documents speaking of these effects were only created near the seventh century. By then, the church had succeeded in the exile of the druids and degrading them into irrelevancy. On the other hand, the *filídh*—regarded as the masters of traditional learning—harmoniously operated alongside their clerical counterparts. The *filídh* tried to retain a substantial part of their pre-Christian privileges and social status. St. Patrick allegedly banned the divine rites of the Celtic filídh and claimed that these involved inhumane offerings to demons. The Celtic rituals were grossly offensive to Christian teaching.

CHAPTER 4
CELTIC DEITIES

The ancient Celtic pantheon—the collection of a religion's gods—allegedly consisted of more than 400 names. Unlike ancient Greek or Roman beliefs, these deities were not associated with human characteristics. The Celtic pantheon more likely consisted of gods and goddesses that represented natural phenomena, such as lightning, rivers, and the sun. However, many gods were also associated with things of primary concern within a society, like healing, identity, protection of mothers, children, fishermen, etc., settlements, sovereignty, and warfare.

The same deities were seldom revered universally across Iron Age Europe and many Celtic gods were confined to specific regions. However, just as there were local deities, there were also some gods that were worshiped everywhere the Celtic languages were spoken.

Single surviving inscriptions of Celtic gods—referred to as *deivos* and *deiva*—were insubstantial to the historical knowledge of their pantheon. However, the Celtic historian, Proinsias MacCana, built a reasonable perception of the vast number of deities, described as a "fertile chaos" (Cartwright, 2021a).

It is believed that the Celts were influenced by the religious application of other cultures. As Rome conquered many European regions, the Celts adopted some practices of their beliefs.

Upon examining the few texts on Celtic gods and goddesses, it is noted that they had a strong influence on the welfare, rituals, and burial practices of the Celts. These deities were associated with all-embracing powers. This often overlapped with the gods of modern Mediterranean cultures. Roman inscriptions of the Celtic gods and goddesses often named Roman equivalents alongside them. This practice is known as the *interpretatio Romana*—the identification and connection between "barbarian" gods and those in the Roman pantheon (Darvill, 2009).

The Tuatha Dé Danann—translated from the Gaelic phrase for "people of the goddess Danu"—is a race in Celtic mythology who resided in Ireland before the arrival of the Milesians and were allegedly skilled in magic. The earliest reference to them states that after being banished from heaven—due to their knowledge—they descended into Ireland on a misty cloud. They defeated the demonic race called Fomorians, who threatened the inhabitants of Ireland. Fomoire (Old Irish spelling) translates to "demons from below the sea" (The Editors of Encyclopaedia Britannica, 2009). According to the Irish myth, the Fomoire and Tuatha Dé Danann were initially allies, and one of the Celt's most important gods—Lugh—was the son of the god Cian and the Fomorian leader Balor's daughter. It is said that the monstrous Balor had one large deadly eye.

According to the fictitious history of Ireland described in the *Leabhar Gabhála—Book of Invasions*—the Tuatha Dé Danann were regarded as actual people by native historians until the 1600s. Popular legends associate the Tuatha Dé Danann with several fairies who supposedly still inhabit the landscapes of Ireland. It is believed that this race fled into the hills when the Milesians arrived.

Irish Celtic mythology states that the Milesians drove the race of gods—the Tuatha Dé Danann—underground. Thus, making them the ancestors of the current Celtic population in Ireland. The legend speaks of the Milesian right to the island after they drove the gods into the burial mounds, translated to 'shee'. The word 'shee' is used by the Irish when speaking of the 'otherworld' (as discussed in Chapter 2) and thus, *Banshee* translates to "woman from the otherworld."

Some of the widest-venerated Celtic deities include the following.

- **Abnoba**, the hunting goddess, who was mainly recognized in votive inscriptions in the Black Forest region of southeast Germany. She was often associated with the Roman huntress goddess Diana. The southeastern German town of Karlsruhe-Mühlburg holds a sandstone figurine of the goddess wearing a Greek chiton. The figure also shows a hunting dog—which captured a hare—by her side.

- **Aengus**, son of the god Dagda and the river goddess Bóann, is also known as Oengus of the Bruig. Aengus is the god of youth and love. This god is tied to one of the most shared Celtic folktales, and speaks of his journey over the country, in search of a beautiful maiden. After finding Caer—who was destined to turn into a swan with 150 other maidens—Aengus decided to also turn into a swan and reunite with her.

- **Aeracura** is a goddess who was worshiped in association with the Roman Empire's god of the Underworld, Dis Pater.

- **Agrona** is the goddess who was mainly worshiped in Britain and associated with slaughter in battle.

- **Ahes** was the patroness of roads, as she was credited with the construction of the Roman roads in Brittany.

- **Alator** is commonly referred to as the equivalent of the Roman god of war, Mars. Alator's name appeared on an altar from South Shields and a votive slab from Barkway, England. This slab portrays Alator as a warrior carrying a helmet, shield, and spear.

- **Albiorix**, a name likely derived from the Roman Albion—the ancient name for Britain—or Albu, is another god similar to Mars. He is mentioned in an inscription from Sablet, the present-day Languedoc region of France, and his name carries into the contemporary Irish language translation of Scotland, *Albain*.

- **Alisonus**—also Alisanos—is a god associated with rocks and ledges. It is most likely related to the oppidum and the Alisos river in Alessia, Gaul. Volvic is mentioned in sacrificial inscriptions on two bronze tablets unearthed in east-central France.

- **Andarta** is a goddess associated with a bear. Seven inscriptions that speak of Andarta were discovered in Die, southern France.

- **Anextlomarus** is a god who Romans often identified with Apollo. Meaning "great protector," Anextlomarus is mentioned in votive inscriptions from Britain, northern France, and Switzerland.

- **Antenociticus**—also called Anociticus and Antocidicus—is a youthful god worshiped at the three altars near Hadrian's Wall. Parts of a statue were also discovered in northern Britain, showing Antenociticus' head and hair resembling the horns of a young stag.

- The glossary of Bishop Cormac refers to **Anu** as the mother of all Irish gods. This makes her a major pre-Christian era influence. Anu is associated with fertility and Ireland was often referred to as "the Land of Anu" in Celtic poetry.

- **Arawn** was celebrated as the ruler of the Welsh afterlife (Annwn). He is a god described as having magical shapeshifting skills and being an excellent hunter. A famous story that refers to this god, involved his changing of places with king Pwyll, ruler of Dyfed, after he lost one of his stags to king Pwyll's dogs during a hunt. After Christianity was introduced to the British Isles, Arawn gained a negative association with hell.

- **Arduinna** Is the boar goddess associated with the Rhine Mountains. The Romans identified her as Diana, who was most likely depicted as a bronze statue of the goddess riding a boar.

- Worshiped in northeast England, **Arecurius** is a god whose name translates to "he who stands before the tribe" (Cartwright, 2021a).

- The equivalent of the Roman god Mercury, **Artaius** was named after the

Celtic word for 'bear'. The god is mentioned in an inscription discovered in Beaucroissant, southeast France.

- Also, the goddess Artio, whose name also means "bear," is mentioned on a 7.8-inch bronze statue found in Muri, Switzerland. The seated figure shows the goddess offering a bowl of fruit to the bear. Another inscription was found in Trier in western Germany.

- **Badb**—also referred to as Bodb—is a Celtic goddess who is the daughter of Ernmas. She is known as a supernatural demon. According to Celtic eschatology, Badb will be responsible for the end of the world. There is a Celtic legend that says it foretold the downfall of the gods and the great famine of the 18th century. The inscription also speaks of Bodb, referring to the Irish mythological cycle of the son of Dagda and the fighting demon who turned into a raven on the battlefield.

- **Barrex**—also referred to as Barrecis—is identified with the Roman god Mars. Barrex's name was found in Carlisle, northern England.

- **Belatucadrus** is mentioned in many inscriptions from the north of England. He was equated to Mars, the Roman god of war.

- Another major god identified with Apollo, is **Belenus**, meaning "to shine." His name appears on multiple inscriptions, literature pieces, and even an engraved gemstone. These were found in southern France, northern Italy, and the eastern Alps. It is believed that Belenus is the protector god of the Celtic pantheon and was often associated with springs that enhance health.

- **Belisama** is a goddess of lakes and rivers, translating to "the bright one." Votive inscriptions from southern France were written in the Greek alphabet and speak of a shrine by Segomaros, a Gaul from Nîmes. Belisama was equivalent to the Roman, Minerva.

- The patron of crafts, mentioned in Alesia, is **Bergusia.**

- **Borvo**—Also known as Bormo - translates to the Celtic expression "to cook". Therefore, this deity is associated with natural hot springs. Devotional inscriptions have been found at the Bourbon-Lancy and Bourbonne-Les-Bains springs named after God in central and eastern France.

- **Brigantia**, The meaning "sublime" is equivalent to the Roman goddess Victoria. Brigantia was primarily worshiped in the north of England, as evidenced by the surviving devotional inscriptions there. A clear inscription identifies the goddess as an African goddess named Kelestis. A relief was found in Scotland showing a Brigantia with a crown and wings - usually associated with Minerva and Victoria.

- Daughter of the Dagda, **Brigid** was particularly honored by Celtic poets as a "triple deity" (Badnjarevic, 2022a). She is said to have powers in agriculture, fire, healing, metalwork, poetry, and prophecy. This goddess was part of the Tuatha Dé Danann. She also had numerous domesticated animals including critters, sheep, and oxen. Brigid likely derived from Brigantia, an older British goddess.

- The **Cailleach** is a well-known goddess with an impressive tale associated with her name. She is also referred to as the Hag of Béara and is one of the oldest and most powerful mythical beings in Ireland. Particularly famous in Cork and Kerry, where the Béara peninsula is located, Cailleach is believed to have the power of influence over weather and the seasons. Her legend speaks of her appearing in the form of an ugly old woman and is responsible for the formation of the Cliffs of Moher and Hag's Head mountain landmarks.

- **Camulus** is a god who was equated to the Roman god, Mars. He is mentioned in votive inscriptions that had been found near Arlon in southern Belgium, Bar Hill in Scotland, Reims in northern France, and Rindern in western Germany. An inscribed stone found in Rindern depicts the god with a crown of oak leaves and ram's horns. Roman Colchester—Camulodunum—in southeast England was named after Camulus.

- **Canomagus** is the god of hounds, often equated to Apollo. A votive inscription was discovered in Nettleton Shrub, southwest England.

- The "king of battle," **Caturix**, is often equated to Mars. This god's name is found in inscriptions discovered across Roman Switzerland and Böckingen, southern Germany.

- While **Ceridwen** was sometimes referred to as a goddess, she was best known as a Celtic witch with great magical power, prophetic skill, and wisdom. According to mythology, Ceridwen used a magic cauldron to brew potions. These potions allowed the drinker to gain beauty, wisdom, and the ability to shapeshift. She was considered a good witch whose potions and spells mainly helped people.

- **Cernunnos** is arguably the most unusual Celtic god. He is portrayed as a horned god that represents fauna and flora, fertility, grain, nature, prosperity, and wealth. Druids referred to Cernunnos as the "honored god"—often connected to bulls, horned serpents, and stags—and Julius Caesar associated him with Dis Pater, the Roman god of the underworld. Cernunnos is frequently depicted in Celtic and Gallo-Roman art. He is shown with antlers or horns, and while he is in a human form, he often has animal legs and hooves. Well-known artworks portray him in a seated lotus position with crossed legs. Cernunnos is presumably derived from the Celtic word 'horn' or 'antler', but scholars still debate this theory. Votive inscriptions and carvings on a pillar under the Notre-Dame cathedral in Paris—the Nautae Parisiaci (c. 100 BCE)—mention Cernunnos. He is also shown wearing torcs on the Gundestrup Cauldron (c. 100 BCE). Cernunnos is believed to be the source of Conall Cernach, the cultural hero of the Ulster Cycle (Chapter 1).

- The name of the god **Condatis** suggests an association with the convergence of rivers. Settlements near these convergences in Gaul were called *Condates*. Many inscriptions found in northeast England—especially at shrines near the rivers Tees and Tyne—speak of this venerated god. Condatis is also identified with Mars.

- The goddess **Coventina** had a sanctuary in her honor near Hadrian's Wall. She is depicted as the water nymph reclining on a leaf on the votive relief of the sanctuary.

This relief panel is accompanied by another relief panel showing three nymphs pouring water from containers. Historians point to this as a typical triple deity in Celtic art. Bronze animal statues, pottery and coins that may have been thrown into the well were also found at the site.

- **The Dagda** is one of the most famous of the Celtic gods, often seen as a prominent father figure. In fact, his name is preceded by a definite article. The Dagda translates to "the good god" and is associated with many skills. According to his legend, he was the father of Aengus, Bodb Derg, Cermait, Midir and Brigit. Dagda has a large mace designed to kill 10 people at a time and bring the dead back to life, a harp that can summon the seasons, and a cauldron that can cook an unlimited amount of porridge. Irish mythology depicts Dagda as a versatile warrior and leader of the Tuatha Dé Danann. It is known that Dagda won the battle against Fir Bolg and Fomoire the Navigator. He remains an important figure during the festival of Samhain, keeping in touch with Morrigan as it guarantees fertility and prosperity in the new year.

- **Damona** is a goddess associated with cows. She is the consort of Borvo, evident in numerous inscriptions found in Gaul.

- **Danu** is the mother-goddess—particularly known from the godly-race Tuatha Dé Danann—who gives her name to the River Danube and other places. Danu translates to "the waters of heaven." As a mother to the gods, Danu is one of the oldest mythological deities. She is mainly portrayed as a beautiful woman who is also associated with fauna and flora. In addition, she represents regeneration, prosperity, and wisdom.

- **Eochaid** is a pre-Christian Irish god that is associated with horses, lightning, and the sun. His name also appears in the Celtic legend *The Wooing of Étaín* in which a high King of Ireland bearing his name must lock horns with the immortal Midir of *Tír na nÓg*.

- A well-known goddess regarded as the protectress of donkeys, horses, and mules, is **Epona**. Epona translates to 'horse' and she was likely venerated in various parts of Celtic Europe, evident in more than 60 votive inscriptions from the Balkans to Iberia. Many images depict the goddess riding a horse—sidesaddle—or sitting on a throne while holding a bowl or cornucopia. The latter images include a horse standing on either side of the goddess. Sometimes, Epona is accompanied by a bird, dog, or foal. The Roman writer, Apuleius, describes a rose-adorned statue of Epona set up in a stable.

- **Ernmas** is the mother of the war goddesses Badb, Macha, and the Morrigan. Ernmas is associated with death from weapons.

- Another god mentioned in the first-century *Nautae Parisiaci*, is **Esus**. While only a few inscriptions of this god survive, this votive monument holds a relief that depicts a bearded Esus next to a tree, a bull, and three cranes. Esus is wearing artisan clothing and uses a sickle to cut off the tree's branches. Roman writers speak of the god as a recipient of humans who had been sacrificed by hanging the victim until their limbs separated from their torso.

- **Grannus** is often referred to as Apollo-

Grannus in inscriptions, found in France, Germany, Hungary, the Netherlands, and Spain. He is believed to have healing powers and is identified with the Roman god Apollo. Several sanctuaries across Celtic Europe were dedicated to him and his consort, Sirona.

- **Iovantucarus** translates to "he who loves youth," suggesting that this god was possibly the protector of children. He is equated with the Roman god, Mars, according to multiple inscriptions from Tier, but also with Mercury, according to an inscription from Tholey, western Germany. A silver ring found in Heidelberg, western Germany, also mentions Iovantucarus.

- Perhaps the most important god of all Celtic mythology is **Lugus** or **Lugh**. Although he was rarely mentioned in votive inscriptions, many places are named after Lugh, such as Lugdunum, modern-day Lyon in France. Caesar describes him as the supreme Celtic god, representing the sun, thunderstorms, and ravens. Lugh is often regarded as an all-seeing and all-wise god, and in later mythology, he becomes a successful warrior and Irish hero. Many have given him the nickname of *Lugh Lámhfada*, which means "of the long hand," referring to his magnificent weapon-throwing powers. He is also called *Lugh Samildánach*, which means "skilled in many arts and crafts" (Cartwright, 2021a). In addition to the Dagda, Lugh lead the Tuatha Dé Danann to victory against the Fomorians—during the battle of Mag Tuired—and killed the one-eyed Balor with his magic spear, called Gae Assail. This established a 40-year reign of peace and welfare. Lugh is the father of the cultural hero Cú Chulainn (discussed in Chapter 6).

- **Llyr** was the leader of one of the two godly families, who were often at war. Welsh mythology interprets the famous *Children of Llyr* as the powers of darkness who are constantly fighting with the powers of light, referred to as the *Children of Dôn*. Similar to the Irish gods Lír and Manannán, the Welsh Llyr and his son, Manawydan, were connected to the ocean. Llyr's other offspring included the god **Brân**, the god of bards and poetry, and Branwen, the wife of the sun god Matholwch.

- **Macha** is the sister of the war or demon goddesses, Badb and the Morrigan. Many argue that she is one aspect of the tripartite goddess of war and death, the Mórrigna. Macha is also believed to be the Irish equivalent of the Gaulish goddess Epona.

- **Manannán Mac Lir** is also a prominent god in the Celtic pantheon. His name translates to "son of the sea," and he is therefore considered to be an Irish sea god who gave his name to the Isle of Man. According to his myth, Manannán ruled over an island paradise while providing an abundance of crops and protecting sailors. The god could give immortality to the gods through swine who returned to life after they were killed. Individuals who ate these swine were able to live forever. Manannán is often depicted in impenetrable armor, with an invincible sword, and riding in a chariot over the waves. He also has a Welsh equivalent called Manawydan, brother of the god Brân.

- **Matronae**—also called Matrae or Matres—is depicted as a trio of mother-goddesses. The triad often holds baskets of fruit and wheat, flowers, or infants, all representing the connection with abundance and fertility.

- **Medb**—better known as Queen of Connacht—was the goddess wife of king Connacht in the Ulster Cycle. She is often associated with sovereignty and was buried at the top of Knocknarea in Sligo. Medb—often spelled Méabh, Méadhbh, or Maeve—was said to have been physically and mentally powerful, fierce, and a respected leader of armies. Her most famous battle is the *Táin Bó Cúailnge*, the cattle raid of Cooley.

- The best-known goddess of war, **The Morrigan**, is often presented alongside her sisters Badb and Macha, as a trio called Mórrigna. Her name translates to 'mare-queen' or 'phantom-queen'. After coupling with the Dagda, she became a prominent member of the festival of Samhain and features in later Irish mythology where she attempts to seduce the hero Cú Chulainn. This resulted in her association with battle, inciting conflict, and as the bringer of death. While it is believed she hovered over the battlefield in the form of a crow and her destructive nature, she was connected to the idea of fertility. The Morrigan was able to predict who would win in battle and when she appeared to Cú Chulainn, he failed to recognize her and subsequently died in battle.

- **Nantosuelta** is a goddess often depicted holding a scepter with a miniature house on top. She was presumably a goddess associated with home and hearth and is mentioned as the consort of Sucellus in an inscribed altar in Sarrebourg, France. This altar presents a relief that shows a bearded Sucellus wearing a short tunic and boots. In his hand, Sucellus is holding a long scepter with a hammer top. Beside the couple is a bulbous pot and they are often accompanied by a canine in other artworks.

- **Neit** was a Celtic god associated with war. He was married to both Badb and Nemain. This god was celebrated for fighting ferociously alongside the Tuatha Dé Danann against the Fomorians. However, he had an interesting family tree. Neit was the father of the Fomorian Dot, grandfather to Balor, and uncle to the Dagda.

- The goddess **Nementona**'s name is derived from the Celtic word for "sacred grove of trees." The goddess is mentioned in votive inscriptions found in England and Germany that indicate she is the consort of Mars. Many sanctuaries at Klein-Winternheim and Trier, Germany are dedicated to her.

- **Ogmios** is mentioned in two curse tablets from Bregenz, eastern Austria. While he was presumably associated with the underworld, the Syrian writer Lucian of Samosata identifies him with Hercules. Lucian claims to have seen a statue of Ogmios in Gaul, depicting the god as an old man holding a club and wearing a lion's pelt. The statue was accompanied by amber people who were wearing chains attached to the god's tongue and ears. The Gauls stated that this signified eloquence and articulacy. In later Irish mythology, the invention of literature was credited to Ogma.

- The Celtic religion involved a Welsh manifestation of the Gaulish horse goddess Epona—known in Ireland as the goddess Macha—called **Rhiannon**. The goddess is best known from the collection of mythological Welsh tales called the *Mabinogion*—also referred to as the *Four Branches of the Mabinogi* (Chapter 8)—where she first appears on a mysterious steed to meet King Pwyll of Dyfed—the land that had a magical cauldron of plenty—and take his hand in marriage. She was later unjustly accused of the murder of her son and was given a punishment where she had to act like a horse, wear a donkey collar, and carry visitors to the royal court. The magical cauldron of Dyfed became known as the *Holy Grail* in Celtic religions.

- The healing goddess, **Sequana** shares her name with the River Seine, Paris. She had an important sanctuary at the source of the river near Dijon. This site presents many votive inscriptions and offerings. Excavations of the site found over 200 wooden figurines and a bronze sculpture of Sequana with her arms spread open, standing in a boat. Sequana's shrine expanded during the Roman period.

- **Sirona** is the goddess associated with the stars. She was worshiped across many regions in Austria, France, and Germany. The goddess is frequently depicted as a woman in a long robe; in her hands, she is holding eggs, grapes, or wheat. This highlights her further connection with fertility.

- **Taranis**—also known as the 'thunderer'—is a god associated with thunderstorms. He was thus equated to the Roman god, Jupiter. Taranis was identified with a spoked wheel and was feared because of his ability to summon stormy weather. The Roman poet, Lucan, claimed that humans were sacrificed to the god, by being burnt in a wooden tub.

- The god **Teutates**, whose name is translated as "father of the tribe," is mentioned in votive inscriptions found in Austria, Britain, and Rome. Similarly, the Roman poet, Lucan, speaks of Teutates' human sacrifices being drowned headfirst in a tub filled with water. The Romans identified the god with Mars.

- Lastly, **Tlachtga** is the goddess of Samhain, often associated with the holy hill sites at Tara, Co. Meath, Ireland. Her name allegedly means "earth energy-spear" (Connor & Connor, 2020). This can be a reference to lightning. Tlachtga was the red-haired daughter of a druid named Mug Ruith. While the Catholics have always described her as an evil goddess, her importance to the Celts is highlighted in a book written by John Gilroy called *Tlachtga: Celtic Fire Festival*. An excerpt from his book states: "When the fire at Tlachtga was lit, it gave the signal that all was well and all other fires could now be relit. The fires at Tlachtga were the public celebration of the victory of light," (Gilroy, 2000).

The above-mentioned names are only a few of the vast number of deities named on inscriptions found in ancient Celtic territories.

Many gods were connected—commonly as a trio—that represented different aspects of the same god. For example, the three mother goddesses, Matronae, signified fertility, power, and strength as individual concepts.

As food was an essential part of everyday survival, many gods were connected to hunting and forest animals. As mentioned in Chapter 2, animals were also regarded as sacred, particularly boars, bulls, horses, and stags. They were seen as totems of protection, often appearing on the designs of armor and weaponry.

CHAPTER 5
CELTIC CREATURES

Celtic creatures differ in type. While creatures such as the *Púca* are bringers of good fortune, the *Abhartach* has a much scarier tale.

These are some of the well-known creatures in Celtic mythology.

- Starting the list of Celtic mythology creatures is the mighty **Abcán**. Abcán is a dwarf skilled in music, poetry, and battle. As a member of the godly-race Tuatha Dé Danann, he was said to have owned a bronze boat with a tin sail. One particular story of Abcán speaks of his capture by the great hero Cú Chulainn. He then freed himself by magically producing an instrument and playing soothing music that made Cú Chulainn fall asleep.

- The **Abhartach** is often referred to as the Irish Vampire and is most likely one of the scariest monsters that are part of this culture. As Bram Stoker—the author of *Dracula*—was born in Dublin, it comes as no surprise that many argue his story has close ties to the mythological creature called Abhartach. Each retelling of the story slightly differs from the one before it. However, the majority follow a similar storyline that was initially documented by an Irish historian called Patrick Weston Joyce. Born in Ballyorgan in the Ballyhoura Mountains near the Cork and Limerick borders, Joyce published a book titled *The Origin and History of Irish Names of Places* in 1869. This book introduced the world to the Abhartach.

The first legend begins with an evil dwarf who resided in Derry, Northern Ireland. Joyce tells the story of a townland called Slaghtaverty. The parish of Errigal in Derry holds a statue of the Abhartach which—in Joyce's book—is defined as another word for a dwarf. Joyce recalls that the Slaghtaverty area should have been called Laghtaverty because of the *laght*— or sepulchral monument—of Abhartach. According to the tale, the dwarf was savage and possessed powerful magic that terrorized the town's residents. However, the people's prayers were soon answered when the local chieftain—allegedly Fionn Mac Cumhaill according to some—killed the dwarf and buried him (facing upward). Unfortunately, the residents' luck didn't change as the next day, the Abhartach was back. This time, he was twice as evil and savage as before. When the chieftain returned and killed the Abhartach a second time, he buried him the same way (upward). Again, the dwarf scaped his grave and terrorized Ireland again. The chieftain was baffled. Realizing he must kill the dwarf for good and prevent his return a third time, the chieftain consulted a local druid. The druid advised the chieftain that after killing the Abhartach for the third time, he should instead bury him upside down. It was believed that this would drain the Abhartach's magic, and when the chieftain followed the druid's instructions, the evil dwarf never returned again.

The second legend speaks of a creature similar to a modern-day vampire. This version includes the Abhartach's death and burial. However, he escapes his grave to feast on fresh blood. The chieftain in this version is named Cathain and he consults a Christian saint, instead of a Celtic druid. According to the story, the saint told Cathain that to kill the Abhartach, he had to find and use a sword made of yew wood. Again, part of the chieftain's instructions was to bury the Abhartach upside down once he is killed. In addition, he also had to find a large stone and place it over the grave to keep the vampire locked in for good. Cathain easily killed the Abhartach and buried him upside down under a large stone.

The third legend was told by a lecturer in Celtic history and folklore at the University of Ulster, named Bob Curran. According to Curran, the Abhartach is found on a small hill between Dungiven and Garvagh, Co. Derry, Northern Ireland. Curran's version of the tale is slightly twisted in claiming that a sixth-century chieftain with magical powers built his fortress on that hill and that he was called the Abhartach. Being a great tyrant, the locals wanted him to leave, but they were scared of his magical abilities and persuaded another chieftain to kill the Abhartach. When the chieftain killed the Abhartach and buried him nearby, the vampire was able to escape and demanded a bowl of blood from the people of the village. When he was killed a second time, he returned once more. Only then did the chieftain consult a local druid, who told him to use a sword made of yew wood, and when he did so, the Abhartach was unable to return again

(O'Hara, 2022d).

- The **Aibell** is a Celtic mythological creature that utilizes music to conquer its enemies. Aibell is allegedly the fairy queen of Thomond, Co. Limerick, Ireland, and guardian of the Dál gCais, an Irish clan associated with Cashel, Co. Tipperary, Ireland. It is believed that she played a magic harp while residing and watching over the humans on Craig Laith. However, the legend states that those who hear her music play will die soon.

- **Aos Sí**, meaning "people of the mound" are creatures that Celtic mythology describes as being very protective. They can appear as beautiful or very grotesque creatures depending on whether humans offend them. After which, they will also seek painful revenge. To this day, Irish people are very wary of disturbing long-standing mounds of earth, known as Fairy Forts, for fear of invoking the wrath of the Aos Sí. This mindset is thought to have developed from a misunderstanding of ancient passage tombs following the Christain disruption of druidic oral histories.

- **Balor** is known as the leader of supernatural creatures, called Fomorians, or Fomoire in Old Irish. This is one of the Celtic demons, described as a giant with one large eye. The tale speaks of noisome vapors of a spell that entered the giant's eye while he spied on his father's druids. This eye swelled into a large eye that granted the giant the power of death.

- Ancient Celtic folklore speaks of a supernatural race called the **Bánánach** that haunted the battlefields. They are described as airborne demons that omit terrifying shrieking sounds. They were also believed to have a goat-like appearance and represented death and violence.

- Another well-known Irish mythological creature is the **Banshee**. This is a very popular character in Irish folktales. The Banshee is a female spirit that appears in many shapes. One legend speaks of her as being an old woman with dirty hair and eyes that send shivers up your spine. Another tale describes her as a pale-skinned lady in a white dress.

Whereas, others still refer to the Banshee as a beautiful woman in a gray shroud over a bright-green-colored dress. Some even regard her as a type of fairy. However, the common factor among the various interpretations is her bloodshot eyes—due to constant crying—and a terrifying wail that acts as an omen of death. This makes her one of the scariest creatures in Irish myth. While some believe that hearing the loud Banshee's scream—supposedly heard from miles away—means a family member will pass away soon, others suggest that each family has its own Banshee.

It is believed that the Banshee's tale originates from the practice of 'keening', derived from the Gaelic word *caoineadh* which means "to weep." Keening is a traditional form of mourning the dead that involves paying one or multiple women to cry for those who are dying or already passed.

- The **Bodach** terrified many, mainly because it is similar to the Boogeyman in appearance. However, he was completely harmless. According to the legendary tales, the Bodach only likes to play jokes on Irish children. Whereas, others told their children that he would capture the bold children who didn't behave.

- Similar to the Pooka, the **Clurichaun** likes to play jokes on people. Other than that, the only information regarding this creature is that it is a trickster that appears in the Irish towns as an old man with an alcohol problem.

- Although our usual idea of a fairy is a happy little mythological creature, the **Dallahan** is a fairy that cannot really be described as a happy creature. Celtic mythology described it as a headless horseman. According to the legends, the Dallahan uses a human's spine as a whip while he rides on a black horse. He could signal death, and, when he calls your name, you are as good as dead.

- In the shadow of the Abhartach, lurks another terrifying creature called **The Dearg Due**. She also resembles the characteristics of a bloodthirsty vampire. Some argue that Dearg Due translates to "red blood-sucker," but this is debated. The legend of the Dearg Due describes her as a beautiful and cunning seductress who drains the blood of her victims. Her story supposedly began when she was forced to leave her village in county Waterford after falling in love with a local farmer. Her father, being a greedy man, sent her away to marry a cruel chieftain. After the chieftain abused and neglected her, she died a lonely death but then rises from her grave as a vampire looking for revenge. Allegedly, the young woman's grave can be found at "Strongbow's Tree" in Waterford (O'Hara, 2022a).

- **Donn Cúailnge** is another well-known Irish myth. The legend speaks of the largest and mightiest bull that roamed the forests of the Cooley Peninsula. The creature is famous for its appearance in the folktale about the *Cattle Raid of Cooley (Táin Bó Cuailnge)*.

The story of the Táin Bó started in the first century, during what was known as the Ulster Cycle (Chapter 1). The goddess Queen Medb of Connacht was a fierce ruler. Her power was influential, and this only advanced once she married King Ailill. However, the competitive couple often compared their wealth and reputation. One night, they called their servant to place all of their prized possessions in front of them to see who has the most riches. These piles contained jewels, deeds to land, ancient Celtic coins, and a vast amount of other treasures. Following a lengthy comparison, it became clear that King Ailill had something Queen Medb didn't, a stud bull with a highly prized pedigree. The queen was furious, yet she knew of a bull in Ireland that was owned by Daire Mac Fiachna. She knew if she could have this bull, she would beat her husband. Therefore, Medb sent a request to the wealthy bull owner in Ulster to request a loan for one year. In return, she offered a gold chariot, the finest plot in Connacht, and 50 of her best cows. However, Mac Fiachna was clever and requested more time to think about the queen's proposal. Thereafter, the messenger spent his time in the local pub while he waited for an answer. Once he had a pint too many, he drunkenly told everyone that if Mac Fiachna says no, Queen Medb would forcefully take the bull. Infuriated with the news, Mac Fiachna sent the messengers back to tell the queen that the bull will stay with him.

The goddess Queen Medb saw this as a great disrespect and decided to declare war against Mac Fiachna to take the bull, even if she had to kill him. Her fierce army was assembled from across Ireland and told to prepare for battle. The queen was very confident in her battle because the men of Ulster were still under Macha's curse—known as the Pangs of Ulster—that forced them to experience the same pain as women undergoing labor. According to the legend, the incapacitating pain occurred every year for five continuous days.

However, on the day of the battle, a fortune-teller named Fedelm visited the queen to tell her of a vision she had about a powerful 17-year-old warrior from Ulster called Cú Chulainn. While Queen Medb was superstitious and thought about what Fedelm said, she continued to battle anyway. She soon regretted her decision when Cú Chulainn killed the first 300 warriors she sent. She tried to convince the young warrior to change sides, which he declined. Cú Chulainn killed hundreds more by only using his slingshot. He sent a message to the queen that he would stop killing her men in masses if she sent only one a day and no one tried to steal the bull from Ulster. Thinking this would provide her the time to find a warrior to compete with Cú Chulainn, the queen agreed.

As the weeks passed and Queen Medb's army diminished, she decided to send Cú Chulainn's stepfather, Fergus, into battle. However, when Fergus saw his son, he changed his mind and they both decided to let the other walk free. The queen even tried to include Cú Chulainn's brother, Ferdia, by getting him drunk and promising her daughter's hand in marriage. The two brothers fought non-stop for five days and nights, Ferdia was able to stab Cú Chulainn once he started to tire, but Cú Chulainn was more skilled and threw his magical spear—Gae Bolga, given to him by the warrior queen Scáthach—through Ferdia's chest. Thereafter, Cú Chulainn retreated to rest in a quiet region in Ulster. However, he was unaware that Queen Medb found and stole the bull while he was busy fighting.

By this time the men of Ulster's curse lifted and she was trapped, a large battle took place but the queen's army was too weak. Although she lost the battle, Queen Medb was still able to steal away the **Donn Cúailnge** (the brown bull of Cooley). Thereafter, the bull fought against King Ailill's bull and killed him, consequently being returned to the Cooley Peninsula.

- Another horrific monster from Celtic mythology is **Ellén Trechend**. The form of the Ellén Trechend differs from tale to tale, but many describe it as a three-headed creature. Some stories speak of the monster in the form of a vulture. Others have said that it is a fire-breathing dragon. However, most stories state that the Ellén Trechend emerges from a cave and goes out to destroy the world, especially in a tale titled *The Cath Maige Mucrama*.

- If any Celtic mythological animals could compete with the fiercest warriors in Ireland, it would be the fearless **Failinis**. This creature is described as a dog who fought in a multitude of battles. The Failinis was nearly invincible and able to conquer any wild beast that he came across.

- The **Fear Dearg** is described as a small long-snouted fairy with a skinny tail. They are closely related to leprechauns in Irish mythology. The Fear Dearg wears a red cap and coat and is also fond of playing tricks on humans.

- During the great famine in Ireland, many Celtic folklore creatures emerged. The **Fear Gorta** is one of them. This Celtic creature is said to take the shape of a weathered man who is begging for food. He is referred to as the "man of hunger" and, in exchange for food, he offers wealth and riches to those that give him kindness and assistance.

- The **Gancanagh** is an odd Celtic monster, mainly due to how his victims meet their demise. It is believed that the Gancanagh seduced both male and female victims with an addictive toxin that gave off an alluring and powerful scent. Unfortunately, those who fell for this monster's charms ended up dead soon after.

- Ancient Irish tales speak of **Glas Gaibhnenn**, the magical cow with green spots. It was believed that this cow could give an endless supply of milk to its owner. The tale originated during the great famine, and at that time multiple mythological creatures were created to inspire hope.

- **Leannán sídhe** was a beautiful fairy known to initiate relationships with humans. Unfortunately, soon after the human falls in love with Leannán sídhe, they would pass away. According to the legend, her lovers were believed to have lived extraordinary lives.

- Probably the best-known mythological creature associated with the Celtic culture is the **Leprechaun** due to its quirky tale. It is mainly associated with Ireland, where these elf-like tricksters are not to be trusted because they can easily deceive anyone. Contrary to what many foreigners believe, Leprechauns have nothing to do with the phrase "the luck of the Irish." In fact, the term is believed to have originated in 19th-century America as a derogatory reference to the repeated misfortunes of the Irish people (O'Hara, 2022f).

- Many old Celtic tales spoke of tribes of wolf men, referred to as **Man-Wolves of Ossory**. Kings of the ancient world used to allegedly seek the Man-Wolves for their aid in war or whenever they had to face a fierce opponent.

- The **Merrow** shared aesthetic characteristics with a mermaid. They were said to have magical powers and were able to roam on land and in the depths of the sea. Like a mermaid, the Merrow is half fish from the waist down, and a beautiful woman from the waist up. These were allegedly friendly and modest creatures.

- Believed to reside in the Lakes of Killarney in Ireland, the **Muckie** is another mysterious mythical creature often compared to Scotland's Loch Ness Monster. When sonar technology was used to scan the lake's fish population in 2003, a large solid mass showed up on the projector and ignited modern speculation that the lake was still inhabited by the Muckie.

- The Celtic dragon-like monster, believed to have roamed the dark and murky waters of lakes and rivers throughout Ireland, is known as the **Oilliphéist**, or "great worm." It is said to have caused the death of many warriors who were forced to fight the creature.

- A Celtic creature that is often misunderstood is the **Pooka**—also spelled Púca—which is said to either bring good or bad luck. While Pooka translates to 'ghost', it was mainly said to appear in the form of an animal—a mix between a goblin, a rabbit, and a dog—with white or black fur, and usually wore a dark coat. It is believed that they can speak and find humor in confusing and scaring people. Other sources say the

Pooka was more of a shapeshifter and could also turn into an old man, a horse with a wild mane and bright eyes, or a human with black hair. A common factor in many stories is the eyes of the Pooka being a bright golden color. The Pooka frequented quiet areas, thus, they were feared more in rural Ireland. They lived in the lakes in the mountains, and these were often called Pooka Pools.

- On the other hand, the **Selkie** is also regarded as one of the people of the sea. They are half-human and half-seal. On land, they appear human and seem irresistible to all ordinary humans. The Selkie is popular around the rural coastal regions and islands of Ireland. According to the legend, if a human finds a Selkie's tail—which they shed outside of the water—and hides it, the Selkie will not be able to return to the ocean. These stories usually involve a human man finding a Selkie's tail and marrying the Selkie woman after hiding it. They also share a similar tale with Scotland's **Kelpies**.

- **Sluaghs** were Celtic monsters described as restless spirits that were stuck in purgatory, as they were not welcome in heaven or hell. Their only option was to roam the lands of the living. Terrifying tales have been told of how the Sluaghs are so angry with their fate, that they would steal the soul of anyone that crossed their paths.

- Lastly, often referred to as **Titania** or **Mab**, the queen of the fairies is also very popular in Celtic mythology. The fairy queen is often described as beautiful and seductive. **Fairies** have been part of Irish folklore for ages and are split into two groups. This includes the fairies who are troublesome, called **Unseelie**, and those that are happy and helpful called **Seelie**.

CHAPTER 6
CELTIC FOLKTALES

The Celtic culture is rich in folklore. Although Celtic culture has dissipated since the sixth century BCE, Celtic folktales are still told in regions of prominent Celtic influence, like Ireland. For example, many Irish children are still inspired by the legend of Cú Chulainn.

Initially, Cú Chulainn was named Setanta. He was the hero of the notorious Ulster Cycle in Irish folklore. Due to his many successful battles, Cú Chulainn is remembered as a heroic fighter and defender of Ulster. To this day, he remains the best-known hero of Irish myth. However, Cú Chulainn died after not recognizing the Morrigan, goddess of war.

As Joseph Jacobs said (1892):

The Celtic folktales have been collected while the practice of story-telling is still in full vigor, though there is every sign that its term of life is already numbered. The more the reason why they should be collected and put on record while there is still time. (p.8)

The first collection of stories was told and translated from Gaelic and compiled as Celtic Fairy Tales by Joseph Jacobs (1892). In conjunction with the oral history knowledge of several seanchaí—traditional Gaelic storytellers—several of these time-honored legends have been retold below.

Connla and the Fairy Maiden

Connla was the son of King Conn of the Hundred Fights. One day, as he stood beside his father, a fair unmarried woman approached him. She was clothed in unusual attire.

"Whence comest thou, maiden?" Connla asked as he was curious where she was from.

"I'm from Tír na nÓg," she replied. "You'll find no death or sin there. We don't need anyone's help to make us happy. For all our fun we have no quarrels. We're called mountain people because our house is in On a round green hill." Only Connor could see the woman and the king and his men staring in amazement at the direction of the voice.

"To whom are you speaking, my son?" asked

Conn, the king.

The female voice replied, "Connla is speaking to a young and beautiful girl who will never grow old and never die. I love Connla, and now I will take him to the Pleasant Plains of Moy Mell, where the Boadag is king. Yes, there has never been a mourning or mourning since he became king." She continued, "Oh, come with me, Conra, her hair is as red as the dawn, and your tanned skin. Fairy crowns await look at you, your charming face and noble figure. Come, your beauty will never fade and you will never grow old until the last dreadful day of judgment." The king was afraid of what the voice said, he heard but Didn't see it and called his druid Corran.

"Oh, Coran of many spells and cunning magic, I call you for help. This task is too difficult for my skill and wit, it is greater than any task I have ever had to face since I seized the kingship. An unseen woman has come to us, and she wants to take my dear, beautiful son away from me. If you do not help, he will be taken from your king by this woman's witchery." Coran stepped forward and chanted an incantation toward the empty area where the maiden's voice was coming from. After that, no one heard her voice again, and Connla could no longer see her. However, before she disappeared, the maiden threw an apple into Connla's hands.

After that, Connla ate and drank nothing but the apple. A full month has passed. As he ate, he felt another identical apple appear in his pocket. Without him noticing, this apple aroused in his heart a great longing and yearning for the growth of a girl. On the last day of the month, Connla stood beside her father on the plain of Alcomyn. The woman appeared before him again and spoke to him again.

"It is a glorious thing for Connla to be living among these short-lived mortals, waiting for the days of their death. But now, the ever-living ones beg you to come to Moy Mell, the Plain of Pleasure. They have gotten to know you as they watched you in your home, living with your loved ones."

When Conn the king heard the female voice, he immediately called to his men and said, "Quickly, call my druid, Coran. The maiden is here to speak again."

The young woman directed her words to the king, "Oh might Conn, fighter of a hundred fights, your druid's power is not loved. It has no standing in the mighty land, where there are so many honest people. When the Law comes, it will remove the druid's magic abilities and the spells that come from the false black demon's lips."

Conn the king realized that since the women came, Connla had not spoken to anyone that spoke to him. Then he asked him, "Do you agree with what the woman says, my son?"

"It is difficult for me," replied Connla. "I love my people above everything, but I have a longing for this young woman."

When the maiden heard this, she said, "The waves of the ocean aren't as strong as your longing. Come with me in my currach, a straight-gliding crystal canoe. We will reach Boadag's realm of Moy Mell soon and from there continue to the beauty of Tír na nÓg. The sun will set, but we can reach it before it's dark. There is another land worth your while, and that land will bring joy to those who seek it. Only women live there. If you want, we can find it and live happily together. When the woman stopped speaking, Connla of the Fiery Hair ran away from his father and jumped into the currach. And then, everyone, including the king and his court, saw the canoe glide away over the ocean toward the sunset. It kept moving further and further away until no one could see it anymore and as Connla went on his journey with his maiden, no one saw him ever again.

The Horned Women

A wealthy woman was up late at night, preparing wool—the rest of the family and their servants were asleep—when all of a sudden there was a single knock at the door and a voice that called, "Open!"

To this, the woman asked, "Who's there?"

The unknown voice answered, "I am the Witch of One Horn." Thinking that one of her neighbors jokingly called for assistance, the woman opened the door and an old woman entered. In her hands were a pair of wool carriers and on her forehead, she had a grown horn. The horned woman sat by the fire in silence and started to clean the wool with violent haste. The silence was broken when the horned woman asked, "Where are the women? They are delaying for too long."

Another knock came, this time doubled and accompanied by a voice shouting, "Open! Open!" The woman of the house felt obliged to answer it and a second witch entered. This one had two horns growing on her forehead and she held a wheel for spinning wool. "Let me come in," she insisted. "I am the Witch of the Two

Horns." She began to spin the wool hastily.

The increase of the knocks continued, and so too did the call of "Open! Open! Open!" Witches entered the wealthy woman's house until the twelfth call of 12 knocks and 12 repetitions of "open" resounded. Thereafter, 12 witches were sitting around the fire. Each witch that came had an additional horn grown on her head. The witches carded the wool, turned their spinning wheels, wove, and sang an ancient rhyme together, but no one spoke to the frightened woman of the house. It was a strange sight, and while the frightened woman tried to call for help, she was unable to move or speak. She was under a spell.

One of the witches directed a stern voice at the woman and said, "Rise woman, and bake us a cake." The woman then stood up and started searching for a container in which she could bring water from the well to mix with the ingredients for the cake. However, she could not find one.

"Take a strainer and bring water in it," said another witch. When the woman was unable to carry any water back home for the cake, she sat by the well and wept.

Thereafter, she heard a voice say, "Take

yellow clay and moss, and mix them to plaster the strainer. Then, the water will hold." The woman did this. On her way back, the Spirit of the Well spoke again, saying "When you get to the north angle of the house, shout out loud three times that 'the mountain of the Fenian women and the sky over it is all on fire.'" Again, the women obeyed and did as the voice said.

A terrible cry spread from the witches inside the house when they heard this. They soon fled to Slievenamon, their chief's residence. The voice—or spirit—from the well instructed the woman of the house to go and prepare her home for protection against the spells of witches, in case they should return.

To break the initial spell on the house, the woman had to sprinkle the water, which she used to wash her children's feet, on the door's outer threshold. Next, she took the cake—the witches had mixed the cake meal with blood drawn from her family while she was gone—and broke it into small pieces. Each piece was then placed into the mouths of her sleeping relatives, which woke them up and restored them from the witches' curse. The woman then took the cloth the witches had woven and put it halfway inside a padlocked chest, one half of it had to stick out. Lastly, the door of the house was secured with a crossbeam, fastened so the witches were unable to enter again. Thereafter, she waited.

It wasn't long before the witches came back and were looking for vengeance. "Open, feet-water!" they commanded of the door's threshold.

"I cannot," replied the feet-water. "I am sprinkled on the ground and my path runs down to the lough."

The witches were enraged and called at the door, "Open, open, wood and trees and beam!"

To which the door replied, "I cannot, because the beam is fixed in the doorposts, and I do not have the power to move."

Again the witches cried, "Open, open, cake that we made and mixed with blood!"

"I cannot," replied the cake, "because I have been broken down into pieces and my blood is on the lips of the children who slept." The witches retreated, while letting out terrifying shrieks, and went back to Slievenamon while attempting to curse the Spirit of the Well.

Thereafter, the woman in the house was left in peace and she hung a mantle of 12 thread colors—dropped by one of the witches—in memory of that night. This mantle was kept by the family's descendants through the generations for nearly 500 years after.

Brewery of Eggshells

A particular shepherd's cottage, named Twt y Cymrws, was located in Trefeglwys. It was named according to the strange strife that took place there. A man and his wife once lived there, and they had twin babies who were tenderly nursed by their mother. One day, the mother was called away to a neighbor's house. The neighbor's house was quite far away and she felt uneasy leaving her two babies at home alone. However, she went and returned as quickly as she could but, on her way back, she was startled by some old elves in blue petticoats who passed her during midday. She rushed home and fortunately found her two babies in their cradle, unharmed. Everything seemed just like before.

Some time passed and the people of the village began to grow worrisome because the twins were not growing at all. The man of the cottage said, "They are not our children."

To which his wife responded, "Whose else are they supposed to be?" Thus, the strife began that earned the cottage its name from the neighbors. Back and forth they argued about whether the wife had let their children be abducted by the fairy-folk and replaced with changelings (Ní Cheairnaigh, 2022).

The mother was saddened and decided one evening to go and consult the Wise Man of Llanidloes. It was believed that he knew everything and would be able to advise her on what to do. A rye and oats harvest was approaching, so when the mother visited Llanidloes, the Wise Man said to her, "When you are cooking for the harvesters, hollow out a hen's egg and boil some soup inside of it. Then take it to the door as if it was intended to be the harvesters' dinner. Listen if the twins say anything. If they talk about things greater than what children understand, they are of the fae. Delay not. Go and throw them into the waters of Lake Elvyn. If you do not hear anything out of the ordinary, do not harm them."

When the day of harvesting came, the mother did as the Wise Man advised her to. She put the eggshell on the fire and carried it to the door thereafter. There she stood and listened. She suddenly heard one of the children say, "Acorn before oak, I knew, and egg before hen, but I never heard of an eggshell brewed, a dinner for harvestmen." The mother rushed back inside, grabbed the children, and threw them into the llyn. Thereafter, the elves with their blue petticoats came to save their dwarfs from the water, and the mother was able to get her true twins back from them. The great strife then came to an end.

The following tale from Irish mythology is a somewhat interesting version of a famous fairytale. This story was originally documented in the 1890 compilation called Myths and Folk Tales of Ireland by Jeremiah Curtin and is retold here with additional knowledge gained from interviews conducted with Irish seanchaí (Uí Ríain, 2022).

CHAPTER 7
CELTIC COSMOLOGY

The cosmological beliefs of a societal group involve their understanding of the origin and development of the universe. This understanding ultimately reflects their model for reality. Think of this as their purpose for the universe, the beings, the forces, human origin and destiny, the construct of time, etc.

Besides the fact that there are very few written records on Pagan and Celtic beliefs, as mentioned in Chapter 1, it should not be assumed that there was a singular belief system that all Celts adhered to. Some corresponding patterns suggest distinct symbolism from a Celtic inheritance, but there are many unfilled gaps, for example, between fifth-century Gaul and the mythology of medieval Welsh.

Many Celtic words, especially derivatives of the ancestral Indo-European language, give us an idea of the Celtic conception of the cosmos. For example, the Proto-Celtic word *nemos* translates to 'heaven' and originates from the Indo-European term *nem* which means 'bend' or 'curve'. This suggests that similar to other ancient European cultures, the Celts believed that the sky was held up over the earth by pillars of sorts. Consider the Goidelic—the northern Celtic languages—word *talamh* which means earth and relates to the Proto-Celtic term '*telamon*' which translates to 'upholder' or 'bearer' (Breeze et al., n.d.). It is believed that these pillars were often visualized as massive columns or trees. This is likely where the theory of the sacred tree that connects heaven to the center of the earth comes from. The title *druid* can be traced to the Proto-Celtic term *dru-wid* which means "to be firm and true." This creates a connotation with the English words 'true' and 'tree', suggesting that like the sacred pillars that hold up the sky, the druids uphold what is true.

Whereas the heavens are described as light and airy, the depths of the earth and water contrast it with their dark nature. It is believed that the Celtic gods and goddesses live in the heavens and the underworld, but humans live in the central region, called Middle Earth. *Bitu*, the Proto-Celtic word, relates to 'life' or *bitotūt* meaning "place of life" where the mortals live.

Whereas the Gaulish term *dubno* and the Old Gaelic term *domun* are very similar to the Proto-Celtic words for dark (*dubu*), deep (*dubno*), and water (*dubro*). The opposite Proto-Celtic term *albjo* or *albho* means "bright flat surface." This connotes the light goddess Albion who personified territory. Similarly, there is also a dark goddess called Dubnona, again acting as the personification of territory, as can be seen in the name of the Irish capital, Dublin (*dubh linn* or dark pool).

A sense of duality between light and dark is reflected here, especially in early Irish tales that speak of the conflict between the Gaelic humans and the Pagan gods which was resolved when the world was split between them. The humans since resided on the surface, whereas the gods were given the mounds under the earth. The belief in this tripartite structure of the universe remained part of Celtic traditions until the early Medieval era. The Celtic triad—sky, earth, and sea—is mentioned in various early Irish texts and tales, including that of the warrior Cú Chulainn. The exclamation goes, "Is it the sky that breaks, or the sea that ebbs, or the earth that quakes, or is this the distress of my son fighting against odds on the Foray of Cúailnge?" (Breeze et al., n.d.). Furthermore, two other words for 'sky' are the Old Gaelic term *fraig* and the Middle Gaelic term *spéir* which suggests "looking up at a curved sphere."

Ancient people tended to believe that the universe frequently broke down and disintegrated, reemerging into a renewed state. Many people feared when the pillars might collapse next and force the firmament down on earth and into the sea. While Alexander the Great wanted people to fear his power above all, when he asked the Celts what they feared most, they replied that the sky might fall on them.

The druids likely had a doctrine regarding the origins and destiny of the world, even though these were not written down. The earliest Irish texts after St. Patrick's arrival suggested that there was great fear of the apocalypse that came with fire. However, St. Patrick promised—as part of a conversion strategy—to intervene and make a deal with the Christian God that Ireland was to be flooded, and thus fire-proofed, seven years before the apocalypse occurred.

Cosmic cataclysm is also mentioned in medieval Irish texts. For example, King Conchobar's oath in the tale of *Táin Bó Cuailgne* who promised to complete his mission "unless the sky with its showers of stars falls upon the surface of the earth, or unless the ground burst open in an earthquake, or unless the fish-abounding, blue-bordered sea come over the surface of the earth" (Breeze et al., n.d.). This terrifying theory has survived into 20th-century Ireland and Scotland as well.

As mentioned in Chapter 2, the Celtic societies determined that time passes during the cycles of the moon and sun. This allowed these societies to recognize the synchronization between the stages of agriculture, sending livestock out or into pastures, and hunter-gatherers adapting to animal behavior according to the cycles and seasons. Many stone monuments of the Neolithic period were constructed to align with lunar and solar events. Later Celtic generations likely inherited that knowledge. This relates to many Indo-European languages using similar words for 'moon' and 'month'. These terms are also derived from a verb translating to "to measure."

Celtic druids studied the heavens and earth to start a new time cycle—the day, month, or year—at the dark half. While the Romans found this unusual, the Gaels of Scotland and Ireland continued this reckoning into the modern eras.

In 1897, fragments of an ancient bronze calendar were discovered near Coligny, France. The fragments are similar to other unidentifiable fragments found near Villa d'Eria in France in 1802. This calendar - commonly known as the Collini Calendar - dates back to AD 200 and consists of 16 columns of Gaelic words written in Roman script. Small holes are drilled next to each word to allow pens to be inserted. This commemorates these days and inspired many timepieces in the Mediterranean world. According to the lunar cycle, the calendar restarts every five years, aligning the lunar December with the solar year. Therefore, two special periods were inserted in these five years. The month and year are halved, naming the month followed by "MAT" or "ANM", meaning "good" and "bad".

The word Samonios, derived from the Indo-European term for summer, also appears on the Coligny calendar. The corresponding Goidic word is Samhain, referring to the festival celebrating the end of half light and the beginning of a year. It is believed that during this festival, the dead come to celebrate with the living. Archaeological evidence from many Iron Age and Roman-Celtic sites suggests that ritual activity increased at this time of year.

When the Roman calendar was implemented along with Christianity, the Celts adopted a 7-day week. However, classical texts speak of an original lunar calendar that incorporated 3, 5, 10, and 15-day intervals.

Although the pagan Irish were well aware of the relative positions of the sun and moon on the horizon at different times of the year, they paid little attention to the stars. Only lunar and solar observations are used as a necessary component for calculating the equinoxes and solstices. This includes a quarter of a day between these dates, known as the Island Celtic calendar system.

Irish scholars were also able to understand the influence of the moon's phases on ocean tides. Their understanding of the sun's movement exemplified the direction in which they moved during tasks. It is believed that the Celts completed their actions the same way as they worshiped their gods, by always turning toward the right in a clockwise direction that was associated with good luck. Whereas, a counter-clockwise movement was considered bad luck. This is attested in many medieval Celtic traditions.

The human head is a common motif in Iron Age Celtic art. Celtic art historian Pierre Lambrechts considers this a Celtic national motif. In La Tène art, animals are depicted with full bodies, but humans are mostly depicted with heads rather than complete. It is believed that the head played a very important role in the immortal Celtic art and literature of the island. An invisible human head is ubiquitous in Celtic art and literature, leading to references to the "Celtic head cult". The importance of the head as the "residence of the soul" is not uncommon, in fact, it is believed in by many other cultures around the world. Archaeological evidence from Mesolithic Europe even suggests that human heads received special treatment after the death of their loved ones.

The human head served different purposes in different contexts. According to the Greek astronomer, Posidonius, the Celtic warriors collected their enemies' heads at war. This practice is also presented through Celtic art; a statue of a warrior carved in third-century BCE Entremont, Gaul, shows the ancestral warrior looming over his enemy who is defeated by the *Saluvii*. This happened when the ancient Celtic-Ligurian people—called Saluvii—merged power with the Gauls. Other archaeological finds suggest that the practice of headhunting was not widespread during the Iron Age, but was influenced by political and social conditions. It was common among the northern Celts. Furthermore, it has been suggested that not all depictions and skull remains belonged to enemies, as some skulls did not belong to male warriors. For this reason, many historians debate the existence of ancestor worship and family relics involving the preservation and display of human heads. However, human heads are rarely depicted in pre-Roman Britain and Ireland. As Anne Rose mentions in her book, *Pagan Celtic Britain*, "It is, however, from Roman Britain, and under the influence of Roman provincial art, that the great majority of British cult heads stem" (2005).

The Celtics have inherited an appreciation and love for the three. Triadism is said to have originated from their Indo-European ancestors and was shared by many other cultures. For example, the Greek mathematician Pythagoras called three the perfect number because it symbolized perfection and harmony. It also presented a sense of "beginning, middle, and end." Some examples of Triplism in the structure of ancient Celtic societies include the division of the Galatians into three constituents, the division of Gaul into three sections, the division of all sacred duties into three roles (bards, vates, and druids), and the three common equestrian fighting units. Art from the Hallstatt period is full of geometrical shapes and abstract symbolism. This includes the frequent use of triplet forms, like three-leaf tendrils on a sword sheath and triskeles that adorn items from as early as 500 BCE. However, Triplism became less common in La Tène art as expected, especially in the medieval Insular (Northern) Celtic cultures.

There is a continuous presentation of triple figures in the iconography of the Remi of northeast Gaul. This is where many coins were produced in 100 BCE, some of which depict three male heads in a row. After the Roman conquest, many depictions of three-headed gods appeared, such as the most famous depiction of the unnamed bearded god. However, the lack of names makes it difficult to determine whether the figures were living leaders, ancestors, or gods. Additionally, historians are unsure of the connection between these coins and later depictions of the god Mercury. The triple head is just one of many to appear on the Remy coin, alongside the "sun horse" depicting the mythical image of a horse pulling the sun across the sky.

To consider this from a skeptical angle, historians ask themselves whether Triplism is a foundational pan-Celtic concept that survived into the later centuries, informative of Romano-Celtic understanding of supernatural forces, or whether this is a new symbolism adopted in a specific region after the Roman conquest and then spread into other areas thereafter. We can see that the general representation of triune deities in Romano-Celtic iconography is withdrawn from the Greco-Roman norms, and this indicates that a different understanding of divine forms influenced them. Triune gods and goddesses, or three-headed beings, were common in the Celtic regions of Iberia. This strengthened a pan-Celtic assertion. However, there are a few three-headed carvings from pagan Britain and Ireland. The few discovered in Britain depict a strong Gallo-Roman connection.

The most highly developed form of triplism mainly appears in literary and religious expressions of the medieval Insular Celts. Goddesses, in particular those closely related to the landscape and sovereignty, are commonly represented in triplicate form. In addition, historical anecdotes, legal propositions, and educational literature were frequently presented in triadic conditions. It is still unclear whether this is due to a climactic point in Celtic traditions, or the adaptations of outer influences.

Furthermore, dualism was also commonly represented in early Celtic art, particularly in works that incorporated symmetrical figures.

Heads that often show contrasting features—referred to as opposed heads—have been appearing in Celtic art for a long time and in a wide region. It also seems to represent specific states within the individual's life, for example, youth compared to old age, life vs death, humans as opposed to divine beings, etc.

Four is also presented as a perfect number in Celtic art. This can be seen in items such as the four-spoked wheel, a four-legged swastika, or a circle divided into quarters. These were all significant to the depiction of the sun.

CHAPTER 8
CELTIC MAGIC

In the ancient world, magic was a common concept. There was 'natural' magic that involved the use of heavenly bodies, herbs, and stones concerning their occult properties. There was also a king of learned book magic. The Celts' most famous tales of magic are compiled in the book *Four Branches of the Mabinogi*, from around 1100 CE. This book includes four independent native tales that are of great interest to modern Welsh studies. These tales, such as *Culhwch and Olwen*, *Lludd and Llefelys*, *The Dream of Macsen Wledig*, and *The Dream of Rhonabwy*, show very little continental influence.

As mentioned before, both the Celtic druids and filídh were associated with mysticism and divination. They learned and practiced many forms of verses, for both blessings and curses. They were also responsible for memorizing old chants, hymns, and incantations. A *cantalon* was the Gaulish term for "basic song," this is derived from the Old and Middle Irish word *cetal*. An additional verse form was the *lay* or *laedha* of Old Irish.

Spoken words, poetry, and singing were considered magical and powerful acts in the ancient Celtic cultures. Certain poetry and songs were utilized for accomplishing a specific effect. Thus, a druidic spell is created by singing a particular song or delivering a poetic speech. Ancient Gaulish inscriptions have referred to these kinds of verses, in addition to Irish text, for example, the compilation called the *Book of Ballymote* was written in 1390–1391. These verses and poetry also formed part of the training at the *filídheacht,* or "Bardic," schools. The Celtic poets (filídh) trained here for roughly 15 years and graduated with the highest degree called an *ollamh*. This is the medieval Irish equivalent to a Ph.D. Those who studied for about 20 years graduated with the *ollamh ré filídheacht*, this privilege was only granted to high druids. In addition to aiding their tribes, they were expected to master all royal ceremonies and act as advisers to the kings. Specialist fields also played a role, for instance, the *Brehons* who were knowledgeable in law, and the *Seanchaídhe*—also called *Shanachies*—

who specialized in genealogy and history. The bards, musicians, healers, and physicians also underwent similar training.

A prominent healer cult is the Physicians of Myddfai in Carmarthenshire, Wales, who were active herbalists for more than five centuries (especially prominent around 1200 CE). The Physicians of Myddfai trace their knowledge back to the gods. Their formation was connected to the druidic—or priestly—services at shrines, as they possessed and manipulated sacred objects that contained supernatural powers and mainly served healing deities. While we are often told that the medieval era was a time of darkness, it was rather an important period for cultures, the establishment of universities, and the development of monastic schools. Great information, particularly medical knowledge, became available due to translation. Myddfai was one of the many locations that thrived due to the newly gained information. Around 1177 CE, the Welsh prince and ruler of Deheubarth in south Wales, Lord Rhys Gryg, was a prominent sponsor of the monasteries in both Strata Florida and Talley. These Welsh abbeys flourished as hospitals of herbal healing. Rhiwallon was the most skilled practitioner and became Lord Rhys' personal physician and, together with his three sons Cadwgan, Einon, and Griffith, was rewarded with properties around Myddfai. These monasteries allowed many Physicians of Myddfai to develop their skills in herbal medicine and—unlike in druidism—they were often encouraged to write their recipes and knowledge down.

Trees have always acted as totems of spiritual identity within the Celtic culture, and many others. Trees generally represented a variety of things, including people—since many believe that people descended from the 'world-tree' *belios*—and playing pieces in board games like *Fidchell, Gwyddbwyll,* and *Brandubh.*

All trees around the world have indwelling spirits, referred to as *deva* or *dryad*. This allows each tree to have its own 'personality' and practical or magical energies. Just like the Welsh yew tree has represented national pride and cultural resistance for ages, also signifying the mysteries of druidism, the English oak tree is symbolic of guardianship, nobility, patience, and strength. The oak tree was the most honored symbol to the druids of the Iron Age. As mentioned in Chapter 2, the term 'druid' is derived from the Proto-Indo-European phrase *deru weid*, meaning "one with the wisdom of the oak" (Forest, 2014). The English oak tree has a root span as far and deep as its branches above ground, making it a prominent symbol of "as above so below" and the shamanic journey. The shamanic journey involves an individual who enters an altered conscious state—or the spirit realm—to gain the power and knowledge of divination. This is the same reason druids held their ceremonies in oak groves. The hawthorn tree is most related to the festival of Bealtaine as well as the *Sídhe* or fairies, landing the tree its nickname as the faery thorn. The hawthorn tree is believed to be sacred to goddesses. The hazel tree is love among poets and signifies the bardic quest for *glefiosa*—divine knowledge and spiritual illumination. As part of the ogham alphabet (discussed in Chapter 9), each tree— including 25 ogham trees—stands as a signifier of a deeper magical and spiritual connection. Therefore, trees are used as divinatory tools that provide a step on the whole journey of life into the spiritual realm (and back, if we wish). It is believed that each ogham tree acts as a branch of the great "world tree" that allows one to get to the gods when climbed.

Here are some ways in which you can practice Celtic tree magic, as suggested by the traditional Celtic 'wise-woman' Danu Forest (2014).

- **Tree Meditation**

Just sitting with any species of tree has intense effects on our well-being. If you practice tree meditation regularly, you will be able to develop your senses of the tree's spirit and become more aware of its energetic qualities. Sit comfortably with your back against a tree's trunk and spend five minutes taking deep and steady breaths. With each inhale, allow your body to become more aware of its surroundings. As you stretch your back against the trunk slightly, focus on the branches that are spread into the sky above you. With every exhale, shift your focus to the earth underneath you. If your attention wanders, gently bring it back to the present moment. Imagine yourself as the tree, with deep roots that allow you to reach high into the sky and keep your center, stillness, and strength.

- **Spirit Allies**

With practice in tree meditation, you might be able to take note of the spirit's presence within the tree. Some suggest you get a tingling feeling of warmth when you enter the tree's energy field. Others have reported that you could experience a shift in emotions or images flashing swiftly through your mind. These are ways in which tree spirits communicate with humans (Forest, 2014). These spirits could take on any form and you should allow yourself to approach any form of communication intuitively, thinking mythically instead of logically. Some suggest making biodegradable offerings to the tree, for example, spring water. Over time, you will develop a relationship with your tree spirit and work together in numerous ways.

- **Wands**

When we think of wands, we think of magical tools that direct the power of the witch or druid. We seldom regard the wood used to make the wand or its powerful properties. We miss the fact that these pieces of wood also carry the spirit of the tree they came from. Think of working with a wand similar to working in a team with that spirit. Thus, the magic becomes more effective. That is why a good relationship with your tree spirit is essential. You will also have to cut your wand (if the tree allows it). While using your wand, you have to keep the spirit ally in mind and use your intuition to work with it.

- **Spells and Incenses**

Trees have powerful properties that can assist you in spell work or making charms. For instance, the Celts believe the rowan—a berry tree from the British Isles—is powerful in the protection against evil spirits. Druids often used rowan in spells, talismans, magical fire rituals, or as incense. Similar to the hawthorn tree, the elder plant—also referred to as elderberry—is effective in attracting fairies. However, you should never bring hawthorn into your house because it will result in chaos. Neither hawthorn nor elder should be cut without first gaining permission and making an offering to the tree. The aspen tree can be used to summon ancestors and the dried leaves are believed to have been scattered around altars as offerings during the Samhain festival. Acorns are used as talismans, especially to summon the Green Man—a foliate mask representation of a forest god—and other gods, like Cernunnos. For luck and prosperity, you should carry some acorns in your purse.

- **Herbalism**

    Many trees are best known for their herbal properties. To name a few, many tribes in the northern hemisphere use the sap of a silver birch tree—traditionally obtained by a plug in the tree when it is fresh in early spring—as a tonic for its detoxifying and nutritional properties. Modern-day health stores sell birch sap. Elderflower tea—also referred to as tisane—is commonly used to bring down a fever, and elderberry can be used as a tincture for colds and coughs—although these berries should always be boiled prior to consumption. Hawthorn tea can be drunk for stress relief and mild heart palpitations induced by emotional overwhelm, and is also used by qualified herbalists to treat heart ailments. Willow bark has been used as a pain reliever in many cultures due to the presence of salicin, which is also used in aspirin. Remember to thank the spirit of the tree to allow its blessing over the medicine.

Just like in the trees and plants, the Celts believed in many spirits that resided in the world around them. Specific rituals and sacrifices took place to keep a balance between humans, spirits, and gods. Supernatural forces were harnessed for the well-being of the community. As mentioned before, all elements in nature, such as mountains, rocky outcrops, rivers, or springs, were inspirited. Additionally, many offerings were made to the spirits that resided in these elements. For example, in Pre-Roman Iron Age waters, many metalworks, wooden items, or animal offerings were made. When the Romans arrived, they referred to these spirits as the *genius loci*. Many of the Roman altars throughout western Europe were dedicated to these *genius loci*. Sacrifices were also made at these altars towards the regional *genius loci*. These spirits included more than atmospheric energy; they were believed to be guardians, patrons, and protectors of a specific place. On the other hand, Roman inscriptions indicate that the Celts believed these spirits were the embodiments of their particular location. For example, the river spirit not only guarded the waters but represented the origin of the river itself.

Filídh rites—like the *tarbh feis* translating to "bull feast"—incorporated a kind of incubational (lucid dream) divination through splashing water, or sometimes animal blood, on the individual's cheeks. These incubation ceremonies involved sleeping on the hide of a sacrificed bull. Additional rites of the filídh can be found in the *Book of Ballymote*, *Lebor na hUidre*, *Sanas Cormaic*, and *The Fenian Tales*.

The Celtic communion with the gods is called the *adbertos*, or *idhbairt* in Old Irish. This ceremony is similar to *yanja* in the Hindu religion and the Norse *blót*. The simplest form of this ceremony includes blessing a piece of food and then casting it into a fire. Similar blessings are done at all festivals. According to the Welshman, Giraldus, the most bizarre and famous ceremony in medieval Ireland was the *Epomeduos*. This involved the marriage between a chieftain and a mare. Thereafter, the mare was sacrificed and eaten by everyone who attended the wedding. Fortunately, this tradition developed into the modern folk culture of hobby-horse dances.

Osteomancy—the practice of bone divination—was common among Celtic tribes. Methods of bone magic differ, but the general purpose remains, allowing the foretelling of future events by analyzing the messages displayed in cast bones. Some societies used to burn the bones and use the ash to predict the future. This is referred to as pyro-osteomancy. The Celts utilized the shoulder bones of sheep and foxes. The method involved the bones of a freshly slaughtered animal that started to crack once the fire reached a high enough temperature. These cracks revealed hidden messages to those who were trained in reading them. Some readers preferred to boil the bones and soften them before placing them in the fire.

In addition, some fortune-tellers engraved small bones—mainly carpal or tarsal bones—with symbols that were analyzed after being pulled out of a bag. This is similar to the symbols seen on Celtic engraved runes and ogham staves, both of which were also utilized as methods of divination.

CHAPTER 8
CELTIC OGHAM

Certain druids and filídh had to learn codes, ciphers, and numerals created from notches that were carved vertically into the edges of twigs. This was referred to as *ogham*. The term is derived from the Celtic god of literacy and eloquence, Ogma. These ogham were mainly mnemonic devices and primitive—or ancient—numerals that were later used for memorization and spelling in the Celtic languages, and divination. Initially, there were 20 ogham characters but, during the medieval era, the filídh developed 5 more characters called *aicme forfeda*, translating to "group of extra wood letters." These were used as consonant clusters and diphthongs. According to Catherine Swift of *History Today* (2015):

Ogham was developed during the Roman Empire and demonstrates the spread of its influence far beyond the imperial frontiers; the fact that ogham has five vowel symbols (although Gaelic has ten such sounds) is one of the reasons scholars believe that the Latin alphabet, which also uses five vowels, was an influence on the invention of the system. (p. 3)

Some regions in the modern-day Celtic world, such as on a hill overlooking Ballycrovane, Co. Cork, Ireland, still house standing stones engraved with the ogham alphabet dating to the fifth and sixth centuries. These findings emphasize that ogham should not be seen as a fixed system. The stones that have survived show new symbols and modifications to older symbols that were eventually lost.

The oghamatic system corresponded with the sounds or letters relating to natural phenomena, in addition to lists of animals, bodies of water, and hills. Only at a later stage were trees and types of wood associated with the oghamic alphabet. These symbols were also associated with different meanings and elements of human interactions.

There is no evidence in Old Irish texts that suggest ogham were used to represent months. They also did not represent any lines found in the medieval Welsh poems, *Song of Amergin*—

many believe this to be the first spoken Celtic poem and is often described as a mystical chant, an affirmation, an invocation, and sorcery—or the *Cad Goddeu*, which translates to the "Battle of the Trees."

Making your own set of ogham staves involves using a set of 20–25 even-length twigs or dowels. A good size is roughly four to six inches. After sanding your twigs to create a smooth surface, you can carve each of the ogham symbols horizontally into a separate stave. According to the pagan author, educator, and licensed clergy, Patti Wigington, the most common ogham symbols include the following.

- **Beith/Beth (┬)**

    Corresponding to the letter 'b', beith shares an association with the birch tree. The symbol represents a change, new beginnings, rebirth, or release from a current situation. Birch trees are often described as 'hardy' and can grow in nearly any environment. Birch trees grow in clusters, thus, what starts as a pair of seedlings can result in an entire forest. The birch's sturdy wood is often used in producing furniture, and its magical properties allow the creation of numerous magical elements. For example, the branches are frequently used for besoms (a witch broom), the silver bark is an alternative to parchment used in rituals, and various parts of the tree have been used for herbal medicine. To name a few, the bark can be brewed into a tea that fights fevers and the leaves can be used as a diuretic. Be sure to only use the bark of a fallen birch tree and not a live one. Beith corresponds with a time to rid yourself of all negative influences. Find the bad things in your life and leave them behind, focusing only on the blessings. In addition, Beith can be used as an assistant in emotional regrowth.

- **Luis (ᚂ)**

Corresponding to the letter 'l', luis shares its connection to the rowan tree. The symbol signifies blessings, insight into the events around you, and protection. Twigs from the rowan tree were often engraved with protection charms, which were then hung over doors to keep the evil spirits out. The inside of a rowan berry reveals a small pentagram when cut in half. Luis corresponds with a heightened awareness of what is happening around you. It reminds us to follow our intuition about the events and people in our lives. This allows us not to become trapped in a false sense of security.

- **Fearn/Fern (⵿)**

This symbol is equivalent to the letter 'w' and is associated with the alder tree, representative of an evolving spirit. The alder tree is often connected to the spring equinox, the month of March, and the Celtic deity, Brân. According to the *Four Branches of Mabinogi*, Brân was a giant who laid across a river to create a bridge for others to cross. Similarly, the alder tree is believed to have been a bridge between the earth and the heavens. Furthermore, Brân head was seen as an oracle in Celtic mythology, thus fearn is frequently associated with oracular power. Found in swampy areas, the alder tree's bark hardens when soaked in water, rather than rotting. Much of Venice, Italy was built on piles of alder wood. Dry alder, however, tends to be short-lived. Fearns reminds us that everyone is an individual with their uniqueness. It allows us to be the 'bridge' between people who are in disagreement.

Becoming a mediator in such instances will encourage others to come to you for advice and a voice of reason.

- **Saille/Siul (ᚄ)**

Pronounced *sahl-yeh*, saille is the correspondent of the letter 's'. This symbol is associated with the willow tree, frequently discovered near water. Willow trees also grow rapidly when well nourished. It represents knowledge and spiritual growth, is connected to April, and while offering healing and protection, the willow tree is closely related to the phases of the moon. Some tribes also connect the willow tree to a woman's cycles and mysteries. Folk traditions involve the use of willow bark—brewed into a tea—to treat coughs, fever, rheumatism, and other inflammatory ailments. Scientists of the 1900s discovered that willow bark contains salicylic acid, the primary-pain relief ingredient in Aspirin. Furthermore, willow wood was also harvested for use in wicker baskets and small curricles. Some bees are also believed to build their hives from the willow's flexible wood. Saille presents the aspect that you cannot evolve without change. It allows us to realize that learning lessons are an essential part of life's journey. Even unpleasant experiences are a natural part of evolution. Saille also highlights that you should give yourself a break periodically and that change will come when you are spiritually ready for it.

- **Nion/Nuin (ᚅ)**

Corresponding to the letter 'n', nion is connected to the ash tree, one of the three sacred druidic trees (ash, oak, and hawthorn). It is known to be part of the connection between the inner self and the world, representing both the transition between worlds as well as creativity. According to the Norse legend, the *Yggdrasil* (the World tree) is an ash tree with its roots deep into the underworld, and its branches reaching up into the heavens. In Celtic mythology, the ash tree is often depicted growing next to a pool or well of wisdom and prominently features in the Irish mythology cycles. Ash still holds a place of honor in Irish society today, where it is the sole acceptable foundational element of a *hurley*—a wooden bat used in the ancient sport of hurling. Nion highlights that for every action there is a consequence, and this allows us to remember that every deed and word we speak travels with us into the future (and beyond). Nion represents the world as a giant web with strands that bind us together, whether it is at a distance or nearby, and the harmony between the physical and spiritual realms.

- **Huath/Uath (¹)**

This symbol, connected to the letter 'h', is representative of the hawthorn tree, often symbolic of cleansing, defense, and protection. Folk tradition involves creating a protective amulet by tying a thorn from the tree with a red ribbon inside your house. Additionally, a bundle of thorns was often placed under a baby's crib to keep evil spirits away. The hawthorn tree is known to bloom around the time of Bealtaine and is associated with fertility and fire. Celtic folklore speaks of the hawthorn as the home of the fairies. For example, in the story of Thomas the Rhymer, he met the fairy queen under a hawthorn tree and resided in the world of the fairies for seven years.

However, even though it has always been used for spiritual defense, some also say that it is unlucky to bring some types of hawthorn into your house. This is allegedly due to the fowl corpse-like smell it gives off after it's cut. Many believe that receiving the huath symbol while hoping to conceive a child, brings fertility and healthfulness. Huath also reminds us that no matter how 'thorny' a problem is, you can use your spiritual strength to guide and protect yourself as well as provide strength to those around you.

- **Duir (ᚇ)**

Corresponding with the letter 'd', this symbolizes the oak tree. Similar to the properties of the mighty oak, Duir represents resilience, self-confidence, and strength. Some scholars argue that *duir* is translated to 'door' (the root derivative of 'druid'). The druids used the oak tree in connection to protection spells, in addition to its significance in fertility, good fortune, money, and success. The oak tree's wood was commonly used during the Tudor era (1485–1603) in the construction of homes and the tree's bark became valuable in the tanning industry, sadly resulting in the deforestation of many regions across Scotland. Duir corresponds with the practice of carrying an acorn in your pocket to attract good fortune. Many traditionalists also believe that catching a falling oak leaf before it hits the ground, ensures a healthy year that follows. As duir can be related to 'door', it is important to be on the lookout for any opportunities that cross your path and know that you will find strength within yourself during unpredictable events.

- **Tinne (ᚈ)**

Tinne, pronounced *chihn-uh*, is connected to the letter 't' and represents the holly tree. The evergreen holly is symbolic of immortality and the stability of family and home. The holly tree's wood was frequently used in the production of weaponry, thus giving it a reputation under protectors and warriors. Pre-Christians believed that planting a hedge of holly around your house keeps malevolent spirits out. Celtic mythology introduces us to the holly and oak kings that represent the changing seasons, from the time of growth to the dying season. Holly is often hung from a string inside one's house to protect the family. Folk tradition also used to soak holly leaves in spring water under a full moon and used the water to bless people or items. Tinne reminds us that there is strength in unity and protection comes with trust. This ogham symbol allows us to develop the skill of responding swiftly to our intuition, learning to adapt to or overcome situations, and trusting our instinct.

- **Coll ᚉ**

Corresponding to the letter 'c', coll is symbolic of the hazel tree. It is believed that *coll* is translated to "the life force inside of you." The tree is associated with August—referred to as the hazel moon—when nuts start to appear on the tree. Hazel trees are representative of creativity, knowledge, and wisdom. Many English pilgrims used hazel wood to create staffs, used as both walking sticks and a method of self-defense on the road. During the medieval era, hazel was prominent in the weaving of baskets, and due to the belief that it increased milk supply, hazel leaves were fed to cows. An Irish folktale speaks of nine hazel nuts that fell into a sacred pool where a salmon then ingested the nuts and gained great wisdom. This myth is further developed in the story of Fionn Mac Cumhaill—sometimes translated as Finn Mac Coll—who then ate the salmon and was imbued with the knowledge of the fish. Coll reminds us to take advantage of our creativity and knowledge, and share it with others. Leading by example will allow you to find inspiration for your creative talent and assist you on your creative journey.

- **Quert/Ceirt (⌁)**

This symbol is also equivalent to the letter 'c', however, this ogham more closely resembles 'q' phonetically. It is associated with an apple tree, often symbolic of magic and representative of love and faithfulness. Furthermore, the acceptance of the quert ogham is reminiscent of the eternal cycle of life, just like the fallen apples nourish the tree and allow the fruit to grow for the next harvest. Apple blossoms feature greatly in folklore that speaks of fertility, love, and prosperity. Quert is often connected to the divination of a love life. It also enables us to remember that we should be open to decisions that are made because they are right, as opposed to what we might want. Trust that while things might not always make sense, harvest the gifts that are offered.

- **Muin (⊦)**

Connected to the letter 'm', this is a representation of a grapevine that is associated with prophecy and truthful speaking. It is suggested that this is because grapes are the source of wine, and once you are under the influence of this fermented fruit, you tend to unwillingly say things you otherwise wouldn't. Muin is symbolic of an inward journey and the lessons you have learned through life. The ogham reminds us that we should think before we speak and that it is better to be truthful than deceptive.

- **Gort (#)**

Corresponding to the letter 'g', Gort represents ivy. While ivy grows freely, it tends to act as a parasite to other plants.

Growing in nearly any condition, the ivy's endless spiral is symbolic of our search for self as we wander from the living world to the afterlife. Gort represents growth and wildness. Additionally, it confronts the mythical aspects of spiritual development. Ivy is connected to October and the Samhain festival. It continues to grow after its host plant has died, acting as a reminder that life goes on. Folklore from the Celtic archipelago speaks of ivy as a bringer of good luck to women—believed to bring a young woman the love of her life when she carries ivy leaves in her pockets—and allowing it to grow outside your home protects your family from curses. Ivy also has medicinal properties and it can be brewed to create a tonic that aids in the treatment of coughs and respiratory diseases. Gort is known to banish all negative things from your life. It is suggested that you should place an ivy barrier between you and the things that upset you. Furthermore, gort aids in finding self-growth and spiritual companionship. If you have thought about joining or forming relationships with others, consider it good luck when your pull a gort ogham.

- **NGéatal (#)**

This symbol corresponds to the sound 'ng'. It is associated with river reeds. Reeds have been known to appear in the creation of arrows due to their perfect form. It is a plant that signifies direct action and finding purpose. It is also symbolic of a flute and its music. NGéatal emphasizes the acceptance of a leadership role. The ogham can sometimes indicate that you need to rebuild what perished, using your abilities and strength to put matters in order and guide things in the right direction. NGéatal allows us to remember that even if the journey is difficult sometimes, it will be a productive one.

- **Straith/Straif (#)**

Corresponding to the sound 'st', straith is associated with the blackthorn tree. Blackthorn trees are symbolic of authority, control, and triumph over hardship. Being a tree of winter, blackthorn berries only ripen after the first frost, while its flowers appear in spring. The berries—also referred to as sloe berries—are known to be brewed into herbal remedies that can be used as a laxative and an astringent. However, mythology has given the blackthorn tree a bad reputation with a connection to dark magic and witchcraft. A ruinous winter season is often referred to as a "blackthorn winter." The Cailleach (Chapter 4) is also an associate of the plant because it is hardy while others are dying. Furthermore, it is associated with the Morrigan (Chapter 4) due to its popularity in the production of the *shillelagh* cudgel—a club used in duals and disagreements—and the concept of death and war. Straith reminds us to expect the unexpected and prepare ourselves to handle whatever comes. Pulling a straith ogham suggests the influence of present external forces. It is important to realize that change is coming.

- **Ruis (𝍘)**

Connected to the letter 'r', ruis is pronounced as *roo-esh* and represents the elder tree with its connection to the winter solstice. The elder tree is representative of the awareness that you gain from experience, maturity, and endings. Although the elder tree can effortlessly be damaged, it rejuvenates easily. The Celts strongly connected the elder tree with the workings of fairies and goddesses. It is believed that elder wood was used to create fairy flutes because of its softness and lightweight core that can be pushed out. Elder trees were also often planted near cows in milk because of their suspected ability to keep milk from spoiling. Additionally, elderberries and flowers are used to brew teas for the treatment of coughs, fever, and sore throat. Ruis indicated a time of transition, as one phase of your life ends, another begins. Ruis also reminds us that with experience and maturity comes wisdom, and these new experiences lead to renewal.

- **Ailim/Ailm (⁀)**

This symbol is connected to the letter 'a' and, while it mainly represents the elm tree, it is also associated with pine or fir trees. These trees all belong to a group described as the "giants of the forest," symbolic of height and perspective. The elm tree has a clear sense of its surroundings and whatever might be approaching. Due to the elm tree's tall growth, they were often used as maypoles during the festival of Bealtaine. They were also popular in the use of property markers. Elm is not commonly used as a building material because it is flexible but, because it withstands water well, it became common in the production of wheels and boats. Ailim reminds us to take a look at the big picture and make ourselves aware of our long-term goals.

- **Onn (⋅∤⋅)**

Corresponding with the letter 'o', onn is representative of the gorse/furze bush. This is a shrub of yellow flowers that grows on moorlands all year long. These flowers are filled with pollen and nectar, thus acting as a food source for various animals. The gorse plant is associated with planning, specifically long-term thinking in regards to having to go without something in order to gain more in the future. The determined plant is also symbolic of hope and perseverance. Onn highlights the importance of continually pursuing your goals.

- **Úr (᚛)**

This symbol is connected to the letter 'u' and refers to the heather plant, symbolic of generosity and passion. The heather plant is a ground covering common in the Celtic lands. The flowers that this plant blooms attract a lot of bees, considered by many cultures as the messengers of the spirit world. Therefore, úr is associated with generosity and contact between worlds. Some folklore speaks of the plant as a bringer of good fortune. It was often tucked under the bonnets of Scottish clansmen before going into battle. Parts of the heather plant have been used in ale, besoms, dyes, and thatching. Furthermore, medicinal use includes the treatment of tuberculosis and stress. When you pull an úr ogham, it is a message telling you to destress. Take the time and reflect on the healing your body needs. It is important to focus on your body, mind, and spirit in their entirety.

- **Eadhadh (᚛)**

Corresponding with the letter 'e', eadhadh represents the aspen tree. Aspen trees are symbolic of courage and endurance because of their durable and hardy nature. Thus, eadhadh is associated with strong will and success. It is important to remember that when challenges come your way, you are strong enough to conquer them. The aspen tree is also commonly referred to in relation to heroes in Celtic folklore, and its sturdy wood is famous for its use in making shields and protective amulets. Eadhadh reminds us that similar to aspen we can bend without snapping. Know that whatever obstacles you face, will pass.

- **Iodhadh (⸺)**

Corresponding to the letter 'i', iodhadh represents the yew tree. Similar to the Death Card in tarot, a yew tree is a marker of endings. On the other hand, the yew tree grows in an unusual spiral pattern—new growth starts inside of the old twigs—symbolic of the rebirth after death. Unlike the other plants mentioned above, the yew tree has no medicinal value and can even be toxic. It is known that livestock has died from consuming the tree's leaves. The appearance of iodhadh does not indicate actual death, but rather a significant change coming your way. In order to make room for the new, pulling the iodhadh ogham tells you to get rid of the beliefs, ideas, or physical items that are no longer of use to you. This is a reminder to embrace change.

While there are five additional ogham symbols—namely éabhadh, ór, uilleann, ifin, and eamhancholl—these are focused on uncertain sounds and are often interpreted in different ways. As you are creating your ogham staves, you should keep a clear meaning of each symbol in mind. The act of its creation is a magical practice in itself. Concentrate on holding each stave before, during, and after completion. This will allow your energy to connect with the power of the ogham. Always consecrate or bless your staves before you first use them. There are various ways in which you can read the messages in your staves. Similar to divination through the use of tarot cards, it depends on what works best for you. It is common practice to place all of your staves in a pouch and, if there is a question, a designated number—often three—of staves are pulled out. As you pull out each staff, you can use the ogham symbols above to interpret their meanin

CONCLUSION
CELTS OF THE PRESENT

Moderns Celts are described as a related group of descendants from ancient Celtic ethnicities who share Celtic culture, languages, and histories.

Since the majority of Celtic culture has faded, the 18th century CE clarified that those who spoke a Celtic language were considered a descendant of the ancient Celts. These languages were most prominent in Wales, and today, Wales is seen as a Celtic nation. This Welsh Celtic identity contributed to a wider national identity that is accepted in modern-day Wales.

However, modern Celts should be distinguished as national as opposed to regional minorities. As said in a 1990 article from the *Guardian* (2022):

Smaller minorities also have equally proud visions of themselves as irreducibly Welsh,

Irish, Manx, or Cornish. These identities are distinctly national in ways that proud people from Yorkshire, much less proud people from Berkshire will never know. Any new constitutional settlement which ignores these factors will be built on uneven ground. (p.14)

This highlighted that Celts should be constitutionally recognized. Thus, six countries have been named and are considered Celtic nations, including Brittany, Cornwall, Ireland, the Isle of Man, Scotland, and Wales, with their Celticity mainly based on shared Celtic languages that had been revived and continued in use.

Some of the most prominent cultural aspects that survive from the ancient Celtic societies include their art, festivals, music, songs, and sport—such as Gaelic football, hurling, and shinty.

During the 1900s, the modern Celts claimed that distinct Celtic-styled music exists within their culture. These were connected to the revival of pan-Celtic ideology and Celtic folk traditions. For example, the Welsh anthem *Hen Wlad Fy Nhadau* is classified as a pan-Celtic song. While there are numerous connections between Irish and Scots Gaelic folk music, the music of Britain and Wales present differing traditions. Celticism is presented through bagpipes and harps, with the harp being the national symbol of Ireland and the national instrument of Wales, usually accompanied by *cerdd dant* or penillion singing. Celtic folk music revival also involved *a cappella,* or unaccompanied, singing and is popular among Celtic choirs. The blending of traditional Celtic folk and modern music introduced the folk-rock genre often associated with musicians such as Enya, Runrig, The Pogues, Horslips, etc.

Modern-day Celtic events include Mod (Scotland), Fleadh Cheoil (Ireland), Fest Noz (Brittany), Troy (Cornwall), and Eisteddfod (Wales). The Celtic Media Festival is also a three-day event that promotes the culture in the form of media. It has been running since 1980 and takes place in a different Celtic nation annually. Furthermore, there is the summer festival passed down from antiquity called *Lughnasa* in Irish—referred to as *Calan Awst* in Welsh—dedicated to the god Lugh. Additional Celtic festivals that are still celebrated under the adaptation of Christianity are Imbolc—*Gŵyl Fair y Canhwyllau* in Welsh—which is currently celebrated as the feast of St. Bridget, and Bealtaine—*Calan Mai* in Welsh—now celebrated as May Day.

Still present at the May Day (Bealtaine) festivals, in celebration of the coming of summer and warmth, the dance called '*Obby 'Oss* is presented around a maypole as the center point. This festival is connected to fertility and a fruitful growing season and streets are usually decorated with flowers and ash, maple, and sycamore tree branches. The *Furry Dance* is performed during the celebrations of the ancient rites of spring.

Celtic art's revival is mainly seen in jewelry. Some are based on the museum pieces discovered by archeologists in the ancient Celtic world. For example, Galway is famous for the production of the *Claddagh Ring* popularized in the 1840s. The early 1900s also introduced *Aran jumpers* based on Celtic fisher designs. Publications on the Celtic art of the Halstatt and La Tène periods were made from 1908–1914, by Joseph Dechèlette, and in 1944 by Paul Jacobsthal. Thereafter, the Scottish artist, George Bain, created hype around the revival of Celtic art in his book *Celtic Art: The Methods of Construction*, published in 1951. Irish artist, Jim Fitzpatrick, then adopted Celtic mythology into a comic strip first released in the mid-1970s. These are called *Nuadha of the Silver Arm*. A widespread fascination with Celtic art gave rise to a Celtic art industry in the 1980s.

Lastly, an interest in fantasy fiction based on Celtic mythology has since skyrocketed in the publishing industry.

The importance of Celtic history is not limited to the ancient forms of art, literature, festivities, medicinal education, mythology, etc., but has survived and developed into a modern culture that is able to share these traditional elements with the world

FREE BONUS FROM HBA: EBOOK BUNDLE

Greetings!

First of all, thank you for reading our books. As fellow passionate readers of History and Mythology, we aim to create the very best books for our readers.

Now, we invite you to join our VIP list. As a welcome gift, we offer the History & Mythology Ebook Bundle below for free. Plus you can be the first to receive new books and exclusives! Remember it's 100% free to join.

Simply scan the QR code to join.

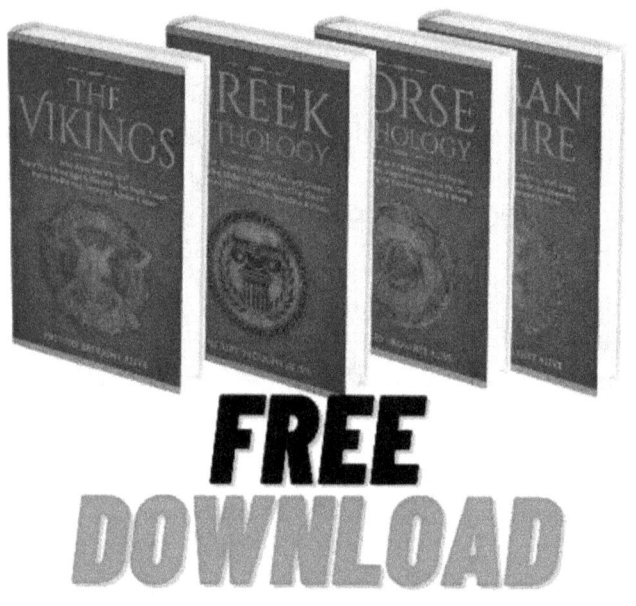

Keep up to date with us on:
YouTube: History Brought Alive
Facebook: History Brought Alive
www.historybroughtalive.com

REFERENCES

Amgueddfa Cymru. (2021, June 5). *Who were the Celts?* Museum Wales. https://museum.wales/articles/1341/Who-were-the-Celts/

Badnjarevic, D. (2022a, May 26). *15 Major Celtic Gods And Goddesses (You Need To Know About)*. The Irish Road Trip. https://www.theirishroadtrip.com/celtic-gods-and-goddesses/

Badnjarevic, D. (2022b, May 26). *31 Irish Mythological Creatures (Tales Told By An Irishman)*. The Irish Road Trip. https://www.theirishroadtrip.com/irish-mythological-creatures/

Breeze, A., Carey, J., & Johnson, D. R. (n.d.). *Cosmology | Exploring Celtic Civilizations*. Exploring Celtic Civilizations. https://exploringcelticciv.web.unc.edu/cosmology/

Ccasar, J., McDevitte, W. A., & Bohn, W. S. (1869). *Caesar's Galic War* (Translated 1st edition). Harper & Brothers. https://www.perseus.tufts.edu/hopper/text?doc=Perseus%3Atext%3A1999.02.0001%3Abook%3D4%3Achapter%3D33

Cartwright, M. (2021a, March 19). *The Ancient Celtic Pantheon*. World History Encyclopedia. https://www.worldhistory.org/article/1715/the-ancient-celtic-pantheon/

Cartwright, M. (2021b, March 22). *Ancient Celtic Religion*. World History Encyclopedia. https://www.worldhistory.org/Ancient_Celtic_Religion/

Congail, M. (2019, May 5). *The secrets of Bull Rock Cave*. Balkan Celts.

https://balkancelts.wordpress.com/2015/10/04/the-secrets-of-bull-rock-cave/

Connor, N., & Connor, C. (2020, August 24). *Solar Festivals*. Celtic Druid Temple. https://www.celticdruidtemple.com/solar-festivals.html

Curtin, J. (1976). *Myths and Folklore of Ireland*. (Facsimile of 1890 ed). Charles River Books.

Darvill, T. (2009). *interpretatio Romana*. In The Concise Oxford Dictionary of Archaeology. https://www.oxfordreference.com/view/10.1093/acref/9780199534043.001.0001/acref-9780199534043

Dillon, M., & Mac Cana, P. (1999, May 20). *Celtic religion - Beliefs, practices, and institutions*. Encyclopedia Britannica. https://www.britannica.com/topic/Celtic-religion/Beliefs-practices-and-institutions

Ellis, B. P. (2002). *The Mammoth Book of Celtic Myths and Legends*. Robinson.

Forest, D. (2014a). *Celtic Tree Magic: Ogham Lore and Druid Mysteries*. Llewellyn Publications.

Forest, D. (2014b, October 13). *Celtic Tree Magic: 6 Ways to Work with Sacred Trees*. Llewellyn. https://www.llewellyn.com/journal/article/2466

Gilroy, J. (2000). *Tlachtga: Celtic Fire Festival*. Pikefiel Publications.

History.com Editors. (2019, October 24). *Who Were Celts*. HISTORY. https://www.history.com/topics/ancient-history/celts

Jacobs, J. (1892). *Celtic Fairy Tales*. G. P. Putnam's Sons.

King, J. (2019, June 10). *Celtic Warfare*. World History Encyclopedia. https://www.worldhistory.org/Celtic_Warfare/

Lloyd, E. (2018, March 12). *Puzzle Of The Bull Rock Cave – Ancient Mass Grave Remains Unexplained*. Ancient Pages. https://www.ancientpages.com/2018/03/12/puzzle-of-the-bull-rock-cave-ancient-mass-grave-remains-unexplained/

Lover, S., & Croker, T. C. (1987). *Legends And Tales Of Ireland*. (Reprint). Crescent Books.

Maccrossan, T. (2002, May 29). *Celtic Magic*. Llewellyn. https://www.llewellyn.com/encyclopedia/article/193

Myddfai Visitor Centre. (2021). *The Physicians of Myddfai*. Myddfai.org. https://www.myddfai.org/the-physicians-of-myddfai/

Ní Cheairnaigh, F. (2022, October 10). Celtic Mythology & History — Interview 2 [Telephone interview].

O'Hara, K. (2022a, May 26). *Dearg Due (Female Vampire): Irishman's Tale for 2022*. The Irish Road Trip. https://www.theirishroadtrip.com/dearg-due/

O'Hara, K. (2022b, May 26). *Puca / Pooka Legend: An Irishman's Tale for 2022*. The Irish Road Trip. https://www.theirishroadtrip.com/the-puca/

O'Hara, K. (2022c, May 26). *Tain Bo Cuailnge + the Cattle Raid of Cooley Story*. The Irish Road Trip. https://www.theirishroadtrip.com/the-tain-bo-cuailnge/

O'Hara, K. (2022d, May 26). *The Abhartach / Irish Vampire: A Terrifying Tale For 2022*. The Irish Road Trip. https://www.theirishroadtrip.com/the-abhartach/

O'Hara, K. (2022e, May 26). *The Banshee: Origin + What it Sounds Like*. The Irish Road Trip. https://www.theirishroadtrip.com/the-banshee/

O'Hara, K. (2022f, May 26). *The Luck Of The Irish: The*

STRANGE Story Behind The Term. The Irish Road Trip. https://www.theirishroadtrip.com/the-luck-of-the-irish/

Paxton, J., Ph. D. (2019, October 11). *Viewing the Ancient Celts through the Lens of Greece and Rome*. Wondrium Daily. https://www.wondriumdaily.com/viewing-the-ancient-celts-through-the-lens-of-greece-and-rome/

Pontikos, D. (2004, August 14). *Celtic Origins on the Atlantic Facade of Europe*. Dienekes' Anthropology Blog. http://dienekes.blogspot.com/2004/08/celtic-origins-on-atlantic-facade-of.html

Rainbolt, D. (2020, March 24). *Selkies: Irish Myths & Legends*. Wilderness Ireland. https://www.wildernessireland.com/blog/irish-myths-legends-part-4-selkies/

Roach, J. (2010, March 19). *St. Patrick's Day Facts: Shamrocks, Snakes, and a Saint*. National Geographic. https://www.nationalgeographic.com/animals/article/100316-st-patricks-day-facts-shamrocks?loggedin=true

Ross, A. (2005). *Pagan Celtic Britain*. (Revised). Academy Chicago Publishers.

Spicer, D. (2020, October 13). *Genius Loci*. Waters of the Gap. https://www.watersofthegap.com/wave-four/Genius_Loci

Swift, C. (2015, October). *The Story of Ogham*. History Today. https://www.historytoday.com/story-ogham

The Editors of Encyclopaedia Britannica. (1998, July 20). *Llyr | Celtic deity*. Encyclopedia Britannica. https://www.britannica.com/topic/Llyr

The Editors of Encyclopaedia Britannica. (2009, May 14). *Fomoire | Celtic mythology*. Encyclopedia Britannica.

https://www.britannica.com/topic/Fomoire

The Editors of Encyclopaedia Britannica, Chauhan, Y., & Young, G. (1999, November 24). *Ulster cycle | Irish Gaelic literature*. Encyclopedia Britannica. https://www.britannica.com/art/Ulster-cycle

The Editors of Encyclopaedia Britannica, & Lotha, G. (1998, July 20). *Tuatha Dé Danann | Celtic mythology*. Encyclopedia Britannica. https://www.britannica.com/topic/Tuatha-De-Danann

The Editors of Encyclopaedia Britannica, Lotha, G., Mahajan, D., & Rodriguez, E. (1998, July 20). *Rhiannon | Celtic deity*. Encyclopedia Britannica. https://www.britannica.com/topic/Rhiannon

Uí Ríain, S. (2022, October 10). Celtic Mythology & History — Interview 1 [Telephone interview].

Wigington, P. (2019a, June 25). *The Celtic Ogham Symbols*. Learn Religions. https://www.learnreligions.com/ogham-symbol-gallery-4123029

Wigington, P. (2019b, September 25). *Using Animal Bones for Divination and Magic*. Learn Religions. https://www.learnreligions.com/bone-divination-2562499

Wikipedia contributors. (2022, September 7). *Celts (modern)*. Wikipedia. https://en.wikipedia.org/wiki/Celts_(modern)#Contemporary_Celtic_identity

Witt, C. M. (1997, May). *Celtic and Mediterranean Interaction*. Barbarians. http://www2.iath.virginia.edu/Barbarians/Essays/interaction.html

Wright, G. (2021a, August 26). *Arawn*. Mythopedia. Retrieved September 9, 2022, from https://mythopedia.com/topics/arawn

Wright, G. (2021b, November 18). *Ceridwen*. Mythopedia. Retrieved September 9, 2022, from https://mythopedia.com/topics/ceridwen

Wright, G. (2021c, November 18). *Neit*. Mythopedia. Retrieved September 9, 2022, from https://mythopedia.com/topics/neit

OTHER BOOKS BY
HISTORY BROUGHT ALIVE

Available now in Ebook, Paperback, Hardcover, and Audiobook in all regions.

For Kids:

CELTIC MYTHOLOGY AND HISTORY

We sincerely hope you enjoyed our new book *"Celtic Mythology and History"*. We would greatly appreciate your feedback with an honest review at the place of purchase.

First and foremost, we are always looking to grow and improve as a team. It is reassuring to hear what works, as well as receive constructive feedback on what should improve. Second, starting out as an unknown author is exceedingly difficult, and Amazon reviews go a long way toward making the journey out of anonymity possible. Please take a few minutes to write an honest review.

Best regards,
History Brought Alive
http://historybroughtalive.com/

www.ingramcontent.com/pod-product-compliance
Lightning Source LLC
Chambersburg PA
CBHW050234120526
44590CB00016B/2086